P9-CCQ-837

S E R I E S

A NavPress Bible study on the book of

ISAIAH

NAVPRESS ®

A MINISTRY OF THE NAVIGATORS
P.O. BOX 35001, COLORADO SPRINGS, COLORADO 80935

OUR GUARANTEE TO YOU

We believe so strongly in the message of our books that we are making this quality guarantee to you. If for any reason you are disappointed with the content of this book, return the title page to us with your name and address and we will refund to you the list price of the book. To help us serve you better, please briefly describe why you were disappointed. Mail your refund request to: NavPress, P.O. Box 35002, Colorado Springs, CO 80935.

The Navigators is an international Christian organization. Our mission is to reach, disciple, and equip people to know Christ and to make Him known through successive generations. We envision multitudes of diverse people in the United States and every other nation who have a passionate love for Christ, live a lifestyle of sharing Christ's love, and multiply spiritual laborers among those without Christ.

NavPress is the publishing ministry of The Navigators. NavPress publications help believers learn biblical truth and apply what they learn to their lives and ministries. Our mission is to stimulate spiritual formation among our readers.

© 1987 by The Navigators
All rights reserved. No part of this publication may be reproduced in any
    form without written permission from NavPress, P.O. Box 35001,
    Colorado Springs, CO 80935.
ISBN 08910-91114

Scripture quotations in this publication are from the *Holy Bible: New International Version* (NIV). Copyright © 1973, 1978, 1984, International Bible Society. Used by permission of Zondervan Bible Publishers. Other versions used are the *New American Standard Bible* (NASB), © The Lockman Foundation 1960, 1962, 1963, 1968, 1971, 1972, 1973, 1975, 1977; the *Revised Standard Version of the Bible* (RSV), copyright 1946, 1952, © 1971, 1973; and the *King James Version* (KJV).

Printed in the United States of America

16 17 18 19 20 21 22 / 05 04 03 02 01

FOR A FREE CATALOG OF
NAVPRESS BOOKS & BIBLE STUDIES,
CALL 1-800-366-7788 (USA)
or 1-416-499-4615 (CANADA)

CONTENTS

ACKNOWLEDGMENTS

The LIFECHANGE series has been produced through the coordinated efforts of a team of Navigator Bible study developers and NavPress editorial staff, along with a nationwide network of fieldtesters.

SERIES EDITOR: KAREN LEE-THORP

HOW TO USE THIS STUDY

Objectives

Each guide in the LIFECHANGE series of Bible studies covers one book of the Bible. Although the LIFECHANGE guides vary with the individual books they explore, they share some common goals:

    1. To provide you with a firm foundation of understanding and a thirst to return to the book;

    2. To teach you by example how to study a book of the Bible without structured guides;

    3. To give you all the historical background, word definitions, and explanatory notes you need, so that your only other reference is the Bible;

    4. To help you grasp the message of the book as a whole;

    5. To teach you how to let God's Word transform you into Christ's image.

    Each lesson in this study is designed to take 60 to 90 minutes to complete on your own. The guide is based on the assumption that you are completing one lesson per week, but if time is limited you can do half a lesson per week or whatever amount allows you to be thorough.

Flexibility

LIFECHANGE guides are flexible, allowing you to adjust the quantity and depth of your study to meet your individual needs. The guide offers many optional questions in addition to the regular numbered questions. The optional questions, which appear in the margins of the study pages, include the following:

    Optional Application. Nearly all application questions are optional; we hope you will do as many as you can without overcommitting yourself.

    For Thought and Discussion. Beginning Bible students should be able to handle these, but even advanced students need to think about them. These questions frequently deal with ethical issues and other biblical principles. They often offer cross-references to spark thought, but the references do not give obvious answers. They are good for group discussions.

For Further Study. These include: a) cross-references that shed light on a topic the book discusses, and b) questions that delve deeper into the passage. You can omit them to shorten a lesson without missing a major point of the passage.

(Note: In some lessons you are given the option of outlining the passage just studied. Although the outline is optional, you will probably find it worthwhile.)

If you are meeting in a group, decide together which optional questions to prepare for each lesson, and how much of the lesson you will cover at the next meeting. Normally, the group leader should make this decision, but you might let each member choose his or her own application questions.

As you grow in your walk with God, you will find the LIFECHANGE guide growing with you—a helpful reference on a topic, a continuing challenge for application, a source of questions for many levels of growth.

Overview and Details

The guide begins with an overview of the book. The key to interpretation is context—what is the whole passage or book *about?*—and the key to context is purpose—what is the author's *aim* for the whole work? In lesson one you will lay the foundation for your study by asking yourself, Why did the author (and God) write the book? What did they want to accomplish? What is the book about?

Then, in lesson two, you will begin analyzing successive passages in detail. Thinking about how a paragraph fits into the overall goal of the book will help you to see its purpose. Its purpose will help you see its meaning. Frequently reviewing a chart or outline of the book will enable you to make these connections.

Finally, in the last lesson, you will review the whole book, returning to the big picture to see whether your view of it has changed after closer study. Review will also strengthen your grasp of major issues and give you an idea of how you have grown from your study.

Kinds of Questions

Bible study on your own—without a structured guide—follows a progression. First you observe: What does the passage *say?* Then you interpret: What does the passage *mean?* Lastly you apply: How does this truth affect my life?

Some of the "how" and "why" questions will take some creative thinking, even prayer, to answer. Some are opinion questions without clearcut right answers; these will lend themselves to discussions and side studies.

Don't let your study become an exercise of knowledge alone. Treat the passage as God's Word, and stay in dialogue with Him as you study. Pray, "Lord, what do you want me to see here?" "Father, why is this true?" "Lord, how does this apply to my life?"

It is important that you write down your answers. The act of writing clarifies your thinking and helps you to remember.

Meditating on verses is an option in several lessons. Its purpose is to let biblical truth sink into your inner convictions so that you will increasingly be able to act on this truth as a natural way of life. You may want to find a quiet place to spend five minutes each day repeating the verse(s) to yourself. Think about what each word, phrase, and sentence means to you. At intervals throughout the rest of the day, remind yourself of the verse(s).

Study Aids

A list of reference materials, including a few notes of explanation to help you make good use of them, begins on page 213. This guide is designed to include enough background to let you interpret with just your Bible and the guide. Still, if you want more information on a subject or want to study a book on your own, try the references listed.

Scripture Versions

Unless otherwise indicated, the Bible quotations in this guide are from the New International Version of the Bible. Other versions cited are the Revised Standard Version (RSV), the New American Standard Bible (NASB), and the King James Version (KJV).

Use any translation you like for study, preferably more than one. A paraphrase such as The Living Bible is not accurate enough for study, but it can be helpful for comparison or devotional reading.

Memorizing and Meditating

A psalmist wrote, "I have hidden your word in my heart that I might not sin against you" (Psalm 119:11). If you write down a verse or passage that challenges or encourages you, and reflect on it often for a week or more, you will find it beginning to affect your motives and actions. We forget quickly what we read once; we remember what we ponder.

When you find a significant verse or passage, you might copy it onto a card to keep with you. Set aside five minutes during each day just to think about what the passage might mean in your life. Recite it over to yourself, exploring its meaning. Then, return to your passage as often as you can during your day, for a brief review. You will soon find it coming to mind spontaneously.

For Group Study

A group of four to ten people allows the richest discussions, but you can adapt this guide for other sized groups. It will suit a wide range of group types, such as home Bible studies, growth groups, youth groups, and businessmen's studies.

Both new and experienced Bible students, and new and mature Christians, will benefit from the guide. You can omit or leave for later years any questions you find too easy or too hard.

The guide is intended to lead a group through one lesson per week. However, feel free to split lessons if you want to discuss them more thoroughly. Or, omit some questions in a lesson if preparation or discussion time is limited. You can always return to this guide for personal study later. You will be able to discuss only a few questions at length, so choose some for discussion and others for background. Make time at each discussion for members to ask about anything they didn't understand.

Each lesson in the guide ends with a section called "For the group." These sections give advice on how to focus a discussion, how you might apply the lesson in your group, how you might shorten a lesson, and so on. The group leader should read each "For the group" at least a week ahead so that he or she can tell the group how to prepare for the next lesson.

Each member should prepare for a meeting by writing answers for all of the background and discussion questions to be covered. If the group decides not to take an hour per week for private preparation, then expect to take at least two meetings per lesson to work through the questions. Application will be very difficult, however, without private thought and prayer.

Two reasons for studying in a group are accountability and support. When each member commits in front of the rest to seek growth in an area of life, you can pray with one another, listen jointly for God's guidance, help one another to resist temptation, assure each other that the other's growth matters to you, use the group to practice spiritual principles, and so on. Pray about one another's commitments and needs at most meetings. Spend the first few minutes of each meeting sharing any results from applications prompted by previous lessons. Then discuss new applications toward the end of the meeting. Follow such sharing with prayer for these and other needs.

If you write down each other's applications and prayer requests, you are more likely to remember to pray for them during the week, ask about them at the next meeting, and notice answered prayers. You might want to get a notebook for prayer requests and discussion notes.

Notes taken during discussion will help you to remember, follow up on ideas, stay on the subject, and clarify a total view of an issue. But don't let note-taking keep you from participating. Some groups choose one member at each meeting to take notes. Then someone copies the notes and distributes them at the next meeting. Rotating these tasks can help include people. Some groups have someone take notes on a large pad of paper or erasable marker board (preformed shower wallboard works well), so that everyone can see what has been recorded.

Pages 215-216 list some good sources of counsel for leading group studies. The *Small Group Letter,* published by NavPress, is unique, offering insights from experienced leaders every other month.

OVERVIEW

Isaiah's World

The Near East, 800-500 BC

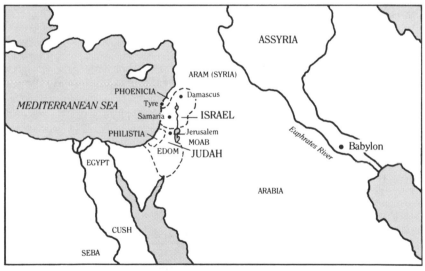

Why did New Testament writers quote Isaiah more than any other Old Testament book except Psalms? Perhaps because it foretold more about Christ than any other. Indeed, if we had only its prophecies about Christ, we would have a prize worth studying.

But Isaiah was more than just a prophet of the Messiah. He was a statesman who spoke God's word to steer a nation through sixty years of crisis. He was a messenger who announced God's desires and plans, and who reminded a forgetful nation of God's character. He spoke of such New Testament themes as salvation by faith in the work of God and His Chosen One. The depths of God's nature and the fullness of His plan for the world were nowhere better revealed until Jesus was born.

Even people who do not believe in Isaiah's God recognize that his poetry is among the finest in all literature. But for us who believe, Isaiah's book is a window into the mind of God as it was seven hundred years before Christ and is today.

Isaiah the man

The name *Isaiah* means "the LORD is salvation," a fitting choice for one to whom the Lord showed so much of His saving nature. Isaiah was the son of Amoz, not to be confused with the prophet Amos (a different Hebrew name). Amoz's family was prominent, for even as a young man Isaiah had "easy access to the king (7:3) and . . . close intimacy with the priest (8:2)."[1] Isaiah was married at least once and had two sons, both of whom received names which embodied major aspects of his prophecy.[2]

Isaiah lived in Jerusalem and was often at the palace. His status and influence at court varied with the royal succession, as the following chart shows:[3]

king	years	Isaiah's position	chapters of prophecy
Uzziah (fairly godly)	died 740 BC	commissioned as prophet	(6)
Jotham (somewhat godly)	740-735	young man; prophesied to king and capital; unpopular	1-6
Ahaz (ungodly)	735-727 (750-715)	young to middle-aged; well known as prophet; suspected of disloyalty	7-12 (15-17?)
Hezekiah (godly)	727-687 (715-681)	middle-aged to elderly; trusted advisor to the king; resented by rival counselors	13-14, 23-35
Manasseh (ungodly)	687-642 (699-641)	elderly; wrote prophecies for future generations	36-66

In this lesson, you'll take a quick overview of Isaiah's career by looking at a few of his prophecies. Don't feel you must study each one thoroughly; you'll come back to them in later lessons. Just try to get an overall sense of Isaiah's mission and message. Ask God to enable you to do this, and to give you a glimpse of Himself as you read Isaiah's words.

10

Uzziah: prosperity

Uzziah was an able ruler. During his long reign the kingdom of Judah was stronger than it had been since Solomon died two centuries earlier. Both Assyria and Aram (Syria) were weak, so Judah's only rival in the region was Israel (the ten northern tribes who had rejected Solomon's successor and formed their own nation). Uzziah's reign brought "walls, towers, fortifications, a large standing army, a port for commerce on the Red Sea, increased inland trade, . . . [and] success in war with the Philistines and the Arabians" (2 Chronicles 26:6-15).[4]

But hollow religion accompanied material progress. The Temple revenues grew, but so did greed and oppression. Uzziah himself was loyal to the Lord, but he did not enforce godliness on his people (2 Kings 15:1-4; 2 Chronicles 26:3-5,16-21). Toward the end of his reign, Judah's time of blessing ran out. A strong king took the throne in Assyria and began to muster an army for conquest. When Uzziah died in 740, King Tiglath-Pileser was about to march southward.

1. The Lord commissioned Isaiah to be a prophet in the year Uzziah died. According to Isaiah 6:1-13, what was this prophet's mission?

Jotham: delay

For the last ten years of Uzziah's reign, he was quarantined with leprosy. His son Jotham was the real ruler. Like his father, Jotham was personally faithful to the Lord but let his people worship other gods and flout the Lord's moral standards (2 Chronicles 27:1-2). Jotham was more concerned with greatness than ethics: even as Tiglath-Pileser was conquering kingdoms north of Israel, Jotham was trying to prolong the time of prosperity. He financed dozens of building projects and forced the Ammonites to pay tribute (2 Chronicles 27:3-6). Evidently, he dismissed the warnings he received from the young prophet Isaiah. Still, Isaiah's social rank, the people's traditional respect for a prophet, and the Lord's protection kept Isaiah from outright persecution.

2. Isaiah probably delivered the prophecies of 1:1-5:30 during Jotham's reign. To get an idea of his message at that time, read 1:18-26. What did Isaiah say to Jerusalem?

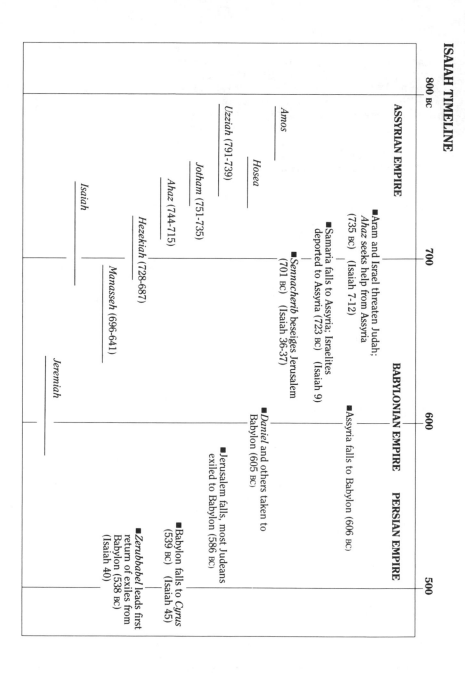

ISAIAH TIMELINE

| 800 BC | 700 | 600 | 500 |

ASSYRIAN EMPIRE

BABYLONIAN EMPIRE   PERSIAN EMPIRE

Amos

Hosea

Uzziah (791-739)

Jotham (751-735)

Ahaz (744-715)

Hezekiah (728-687)

Isaiah

Manasseh (696-641)

Jeremiah

■ Aram and Israel threaten Judah;
Ahaz seeks help from Assyria
(735 BC) (Isaiah 7-12)

■ Samaria falls to Assyria; Israelites
deported to Assyria (723 BC) (Isaiah 9)

■ Sennacherib beseiges Jerusalem
(701 BC) (Isaiah 36-37)

■ Assyria falls to Babylon (606 BC)

■ Daniel and others taken to
Babylon (605 BC)

■ Jerusalem falls, most Judeans
exiled to Babylon (586 BC)

■ Babylon falls to Cyrus
(539 BC) (Isaiah 45)

■ Zerubbabel leads first
return of exiles from
Babylon (538 BC)
(Isaiah 40)

12

_____

_____

_____

_____

_____

Ahaz: folly

Ahaz succeeded his father in a time of decision. He failed the test. The kings of Syria and Israel were allying to resist the Assyrian onslaught. They threatened to invade Judah unless Ahaz agreed to join them. Ahaz didn't know whether to be more terrified of Assyria or of Syria and Israel, but he decided he was smart enough to use Assyria against his nearer rivals without being squashed along with them. Isaiah warned Ahaz not to seek help from Assyria (7:1-8:22), but he was ignored. Ahaz cried out to Tiglath-Pileser, who obliged by sacking and deporting Gaza, Syria, and most of Israel by 732 BC. For the favor, Tiglath-Pileser extracted a huge tribute from Judah and summoned Ahaz to pledge his loyalty.

On his way to Assyria, Ahaz saw an altar in Damascus that he liked (art connoisseur that he was), so he had plans sent to Jerusalem. He set up this new altar in the Lord's Temple and on it sacrificed to Syrian gods. The old altar of the Lord he moved aside and used for divination (the Assyrian method of seeking divine guidance by studying the entrails of sacrificial victims). Eventually, Ahaz closed the Temple and authorized full-scale idolatry. He even burned his own sons in child sacrifice (2 Kings 16:1-20, 2 Chronicles 28:1-27).

3. Isaiah spoke 7:1-12:6 at various times during Ahaz's reign. What counsel did he give Ahaz when Syria and Israel threatened (7:3-4,9)?

_____

_____

_____

_____

_____

4. How did God encourage Isaiah during this crisis?

8:11-15 _____

9:2-7 _____

Hezekiah: hope

Hezekiah was a different character from his father Ahaz. He was a bold patriot, dedicated to Judah's welfare. He also had a healthy respect for both the Lord and His prophet, who was some fifteen years older than Hezekiah (Isaiah was about forty years old when Hezekiah took the throne). Because the new king was eager to listen to Isaiah and to know the Lord, Isaiah was able to influence national policies at crucial moments (2 Kings 18:1-20:21, 2 Chronicles 29:1-32:33).

Hezekiah began by trying to stamp out idolatry in Judah. He had the Temple reopened and cleansed of pagan objects. He banned idolatry and ordered pagan worship sites destroyed. He even invited the tiny remnant of Israel to join in a Passover celebration. But Israel was a lost cause: its king rebelled against Assyria, and the new Assyrian king, Sargon, responded with a brutal siege. In 721 BC, Sargon took Israel's capital, deported 27,292 of the nation's prominent people,[5] and replaced them with conquered pagans from elsewhere. Israel was obliterated, and Judah escaped only by paying harsh tribute.

Another crisis occurred in 703, when Hezekiah fell deathly ill. Since he had no son, the line of David was in danger. But Hezekiah prayed, and he was spared for fifteen years (Isaiah 38).

At that time, one Merodach-Baladan managed to wrest Babylon from Assyrian rule. To visit Jerusalem, he grasped the excuse of congratulating Hezekiah on his recovery from illness. His real errand was to urge an alliance against Assyria. The alliance came to nothing, but the visit was a portent of things to come (Isaiah 39).

The great crisis began in 705 and ended in 701. When Sennacherib followed Sargon as king of Assyria, many subject countries decided to revolt against their unbearable tribute payments. Hezekiah the patriot determined to join them. Isaiah fought in vain against a faction at court who urged

Hezekiah to ally with Egypt against Assyria (Isaiah 28-31). Sennacherib was merciless. In 701 he led his army in a campaign of terror down the west coast of Palestine and began to march on Jerusalem. Hezekiah panicked. He began to empty even the palace and Temple of riches to placate Sennacherib, but the Assyrian was determined to level Jerusalem. Only the Lord's intervention prevented him from taking the Holy City, and only Isaiah's prophecies kept Hezekiah from crumbling under pressure (Isaiah 36-37).

5. When some of Hezekiah's counselors advised him to join Egypt against Assyria, what was Isaiah's word from God (30:1-5,15-18)?

_____

_____

_____

_____

_____

6. Because Hezekiah ignored Isaiah, Sennacherib invaded Judah. What message did the Lord give in Hezekiah's desperate hour (37:30-35)?

_____

_____

_____

_____

_____

Into the future

Just a pitiful remnant of Judah survived the onslaught of 701 BC, but it was enough to preserve the nation for another century. The Lord had planned Babylon, not Assyria, to be Judah's captor.

The last twenty-seven chapters of Isaiah's book look beyond immediate events into the centuries to come. He probably wrote them for future generations rather than spoke them to his contemporaries. As an old man he compiled his visions as a warning and encouragement for posterity.

A Babylonian king named Nebuchadnezzar defeated the Assyrian army in 606 BC. His army subdued Syria and Palestine, and carried a number of Judah's noblemen back to Babylon. Eighteen years later, after some annoying revolts, Nebuchadnezzar leveled Jerusalem and brought the rest of her people to Babylon. For seventy years Judah was deserted. Then a Persian named Cyrus began to weld an empire and finally took Babylon in 539. It was his policy to return deported peoples to their lands in order to seek the favor of their gods. Accordingly, he restored the Jews to Judah and authorized them to rebuild their Temple. The Lord revealed these events to Isaiah toward the end of his life, centuries before they occurred (Isaiah 40-66).

But He showed Isaiah still more. At various places in his book, but especially in the second section, Isaiah recorded revelations of the more distant future—of the King who would come to suffer for and reign over not just Judah, but all the earth. The Lord sent Isaiah not just as a statesman for his own age, but as a herald of the most awesome plans in the heart of God.[6]

7. What encouragement did God prepare for the exiled Jews a century before they were born?

40:1-5 _____

_____

_____

_____

_____

45:1-4 _____

_____

_____

_____

8. What further promises did the Lord reveal through Isaiah?

42:1-4 _____

_____

_____

_____

65:17-19 _____

_____

_____

_____

_____

9. You've had a whirlwind tour of Isaiah's book. Much of it you may not understand. If so, don't worry. What are your first impressions of Isaiah and his message? (First impressions may include Isaiah's style, topics, emotions, attitudes toward God and the people of Judah, etc.)

_____

_____

_____

_____

_____

_____

Study Skill—Application

The last step of Bible study is asking yourself, "What difference should this passage make to my life? How should it make me want to think or act?" Application will require time, thought, prayer, and perhaps even discussion with another person.

You may sometimes find it more productive to concentrate on one specific application, giving it careful thought and prayer, than to list several potential applications without really reflecting on them or committing yourself to them. At other times, you may want to list many implications that a passage has for your life. Then you can choose one or two of these to act or meditate upon.

Sometimes you will immediately see what you need to do about what you have learned from God's Word. At other times, the only obvious response will be prayer—perhaps praise, thanks, confession, or petition. If so, you may find it fruitful to plan to pray about the same passage daily for several days. In this way, the truths of the passage may sink in and remain with you, and you may see it affecting your life.

10. Is there any response you would like to make to something you observed in Isaiah's book? If so, jot down your thoughts and plans.

_____

_____

_____

_____

_____

17

_____

_____

_____

11. If you have any questions about the historical background or the passages in this lesson, record them here. Also, write down any questions about the book of Isaiah that you would like to answer as you study. (The resources listed on pages 213-216 may help you with some of your immediate questions.)

_____

_____

_____

_____

Isaiah's book

The book of Isaiah is a collection of prophecies organized into two main sections, each composed of smaller sections. Here is a possible outline of the book:[7]

Part 1: The Book of Judgment (chapters 1-39)
  I. Rebuke and Promise (1:1-6:13)
    A. Introduction: Judah Charged with Breaking the Covenant (1:1-31)
    B. The Future of Judah and Jerusalem (2:1-4:6)
      1. Jerusalem's future glory (2:1-5)
      2. Judah's future discipline (2:6-4:1)
      3. Jerusalem's future restoration (4:2-6)
    C. Judah Sentenced to Judgment and Exile (5:1-30)
    D. Isaiah's Commission (6:1-13)

  II. The Threat against Judah in 735 BC (7:1-12:6)
    A. Ahaz Warned Not to Fear the Alliance (7:1-25)
    B. Isaiah's Son and David's Son (8:1-9:7)
    C. Judgment against Israel (9:8-10:4)
    D. The Destruction of Assyria (10:5-34)
    E. The Davidic King and Kingdom (11:1-16)
    F. Songs of Joy for Deliverance (12:1-6)

  III. Judgment against the Nations (13:1-23:18)
    A. Babylon (13:1-14:23)
    B. Assyria (14:24-27)

18

For the group

Worship. At least a brief period of worship is a good way to bring people into the mood of listening to God in Bible study. This can be as brief as a song or an opening prayer for guidance, or as long as you like. Some groups like to begin with a brief prayer and song, and end with more extensive prayer for members' concerns. Other groups prefer to spend considerable time in song and prayer before studying.

Warm-up. People often find it hard to dive straight into a Bible discussion while their thoughts are still on what they did during the day. Starting with singing or prayer can help people make the transition from business to Bible study, but many groups like to begin with a brief warm-up question.

As you start a new study, whether the group has been together for a long time or has many new members, you may want to talk about what each group member hopes to get out of your group—out of your study of Isaiah, and out of whatever else you might do together. How much emphasis would you like to put on prayer, study, outreach to others, singing, sharing, and so on? What are your goals for personal growth, service to others, etc.? If you have someone write down each member's hopes and expectations, then you can look back at these goals later to see if they are being met. You might discuss what you each hope to *give* as well as *get* in your group.

You can take a whole meeting to do this before you begin to study Isaiah, or you can take fifteen minutes to do it at the beginning of your discussion of lesson one.

How to Use This Study. Make sure the group is committed to preparing each lesson ahead of time. Point out the optional questions, the Study Skills, and the "Study Aids" appendix. If necessary, examine how members' goals for the group can be met; for instance, do you need to allow two weeks per lesson in order to save more time for prayer and sharing? Address any questions the group has about the study.

Your group members may wish for space to write answers to the optional questions. In particular, those who have been studying the Bible for a long time may find the marginal questions more interesting than the numbered ones, so the lack of space may be frustrating. However, we have made many of the deeper questions optional so as to let you choose which topics to pursue. Anyone who wants to write answers to the optional questions can do so in a separate notebook. A notebook is also useful for planning applications, recording prayer requests from the group, and taking notes from your discussions. Encourage your group to get notebooks.

Overview. The best way to begin studying a book is to read it all the way through. However, we suspect that few people will want to read all of Isaiah in one week. So, the background and questions in this lesson are meant to give you at least a partial overview of the book.

To refresh the group's memories, ask a few questions about the background material, such as:

Who was Isaiah? What do you know about him?
Who was Uzziah? What was life like in Judah when he was king? What happened to Isaiah during the last year of Uzziah's life? (This last question will lead you into discussing question 1.)
Who was Jotham? What kind of a person was he? What was happening in Judah during his reign? What was Isaiah's message at that time (question 2)?
Who was Ahaz? . . . (questions 3 and 4)?
Who was Hezekiah? . . . (questions 5 and 6)?
What near future events did Isaiah foresee in chapters 40-66 of his book? What distant future events did he foresee? (Questions 7 and 8 fit here.)

Now give everyone a chance to share first impressions and questions about the book (questions 9 and 11). Try to get a sense of Isaiah as a person, what his overall mission and message were, and how his message developed over the years.

Application. You may find it hard to think of specific ways Isaiah applies to your lives after just this brief overview, especially if the group is not used to making specific applications. If the idea is new to some group members, try thinking of some examples together. List some general ways in which the book is relevant today. Then think of some ways of responding in prayer or action (question 10).

Wrap-up. The group leader should have read through lesson two and its "For the group" section. At this point, he or she can give a short summary of what members can expect in that lesson and the coming meeting. This is a chance to whet everyone's appetite, omit any numbered questions, assign any optional questions, or forewarn members of possible difficulties.

Encourage anyone who found the overview especially hard. Some people are better at seeing the big picture or the whole of a book than others. Some are best at analyzing a particular verse or paragraph, while others are strongest at seeing how a passage applies to our lives. Urge members to give thanks for their own and others' strengths, and to give and request help when needed. The group is a place to learn from each other. Later lessons will draw on the gifts of close analyzers as well as overviewers and appliers, practical as well as theoretical thinkers.

However, an eighteen-week study of Isaiah has to be more of an overview than a twelve-week study of a New Testament epistle. Those who have done much close verse analysis of the New Testament, but little study in the Prophets, will find that this study demands new skills. Encourage everyone to find his or her own level of depth. Some members will be able to digest only part of each lesson, while others will find the observation questions easy and prefer to spend time on the thought questions. The group leader needs to assess the group and gear the discussion appropriately.

Worship. Take some time to praise God for what He reveals about Himself in the passages you have studied. Thank Him for His Word through the prophets, and for what He is doing in each of your lives.

1. George L. Robinson, "Isaiah," *the International Standard Bible Encyclopaedia*, volume 3 (Grand Rapids, Michigan: William B. Eerdmans Publishing Company, 1956), page 1495.
2. According to Herbert Wolf and John H. Stek, "Isaiah," *The NIV Study Bible*, edited by Kenneth Barker (Grand Rapids, Michigan: Zondervan Corporation, 1985), page 1027, Isaiah's first wife may have died and his second son may have been born of a second wife. See also Robinson, page 1495.
3. The dates given are from *The NIV Study Bible*; J. I. Packer, Merrill C. Tenney, and William White, Jr., *The World of the Old Testament* (Nashville: Thomas Nelson Publishers, 1982), page 62; and Robinson, page 1496. Packer, Tenney, and White give an excellent summary of the difficulty of sorting out the dates of kings with overlapping reigns, pages 33-66. It was common for sons to co-reign with their aging fathers, and the Bible assigns those overlapping years to both kings. Therefore, it is hard to pinpoint the starting and ending years. For simplicity, we have credited overlapping years to the father.
   The dates in parentheses are those that many other scholars support.
4. Robinson, page 1496. In 2 Kings, Uzziah is also called Azariah. According to *The NIV Study Bible*, page 653, Azariah was probably his personal name, and Uzziah was his "throne name." Men often took new names when they became kings.
5. Sargon recorded this exact number on a pillar to boast of his successes, according to Robinson, page 1496. *The NIV Study Bible*, page 556, gives the number as 27,290.
6. The scriptural account of the reigns of Uzziah, Jotham, Ahaz, Hezekiah, and Manasseh is in 2 Kings 15:1-21:18. The rest of this history is from Robinson; and Derek Kidner, "Isaiah," *The New Bible Commentary: Revised*, edited by Guthrie, et al. (Grand Rapids, Michigan: William B. Eerdmans Publishing Company, 1970), page 588.
7. This outline is adapted from *The NIV Study Bible*, pages 1016-1017; H. C. Leupold, *Exposition of Isaiah* (Grand Rapids, Michigan: Baker Book House, 1968), volume 1, pages 38-47, and volume 2, pages 7-16.

ISAIAH 1:1-31

Rebels

Isaiah doesn't begin his book with his vision of the Lord calling him to be a prophet (6:1-13). Instead, he leads up to it with 1:1-5:30, prophecies that show the reason for his startling commission. Chapter 1 begins this opening section and in fact summarizes the whole book. Therefore, we've allowed a whole lesson for this one chapter.

Before you begin the questions below, read 1:1-31 carefully. Ask the Lord to guide you as you look for His message to Judah and to you.

Hear, O heavens! Listen, O earth! (1:2). The Law of Moses required two witnesses to convict a person of a crime. Therefore, when the Lord established His covenant with Israel, He called the heavens and the earth as the two witnesses who would testify that Israel had promised to love and obey Him (Deuteronomy 19:15, 30:19, 31:28, 32:1). Now the Lord calls His witnesses to review the evidence against Israel, so that they can testify that the people have broken their part of the covenant, while the Lord has kept His part. You will notice a lot of legal language in Isaiah's prophecies.

Daughter of Zion (1:8). Zion is the mountain on which Jerusalem is built. The prophets and psalmists often portray the people of Jerusalem collectively as a young woman.

23

For Thought and Discussion: a. Why was the Lord not pleased with His people even though they were obeying His laws of worship (1:11-17)?

b. How might 1:11-17 be relevant to Christian worshipers?

Sodom . . . Gomorrah (1:10). Two cities that the Lord utterly destroyed because of their unrepentant wickedness (Genesis 18:20-21; 19:5,24-25).

1. Observe how God described the people of Judah and Jerusalem in 1:1-31. What do these names tell you about their relationship to Him and about how He regarded them?

[my] children (1:2), my people (1:3) _____

_____

_____

_____

_____

brood of evildoers (1:4), people of Gomorrah (1:10), harlot (1:21)

_____

_____

_____

_____

Sacrifices (1:11-14). God's Law commanded all of the religious acts described in 1:11-14—the burning of animal sacrifices and incense, offerings of agricultural produce, the weekly Sabbath, festivals on the New Moon of each month, and the annual feasts of Passover, Weeks, and Tabernacles.

Fatherless (1:17). These were the most vulnerable members of society, so they became symbolic of anyone powerless to defend himself. *Widows* and fatherless children were easily defrauded because only males could take legal action, make contracts, and manage property. Also, a family without men to help work the land was often poor.[1]

24

Sacred oaks . . . gardens (1:29). God had commanded the Israelites to stamp out the practices
of the Canaanites, but instead Israel[2] had
adopted those practices alongside the worship
of the Lord. The people sought the power of
divine (demonic) beings who dwelt in sacred
trees and gardens.

**Optional
Application:** a. What
would be some mod-
ern parallels for the
sins you named in
question 2?
b. Do you practice
any habits like these?
Talk with God about
this.

2. How had the people of Judah sinned against
their Lord and Father?

1:2,4 _____

_____

_____

1:3 _____

_____

_____

1:15-17,23 _____

_____

_____

_____

1:29 _____

_____

_____

Desolate (1:7). If this prophecy dates from early in
Isaiah's ministry, then he may have foreseen the
desolation that came during the next few
decades. Aram, the northern kingdom of Israel,
Edom, and Philistia all invaded Judah between
740 and 730 BC; Assyria devastated most of the
country in 701; Babylon finished the job in 605.

Shelter . . . hut (1:8). When their fruit was ripe,
farmers would set up temporary huts in their
fields and vineyards. They would spend the

25

Optional Application: a. Are people today faced with a choice like the one you described in question 4? If so, what should we do in light of that choice?
    b. Specifically what should you do?

night in the huts, watching for thieving people and animals. After the harvest, such huts were abandoned to decay in the rainy season.[3]

3. What were the consequences of persistent rebellion (1:5-6,7-8,15)?

_____

_____

_____

_____

_____

Eat . . . be devoured (1:19-20). To emphasize the contrast, these are the same Hebrew verb: "eat . . . be eaten."

Turn . . . restore (1:25-26). Again, the same Hebrew word in each case.[4]

4. What two alternatives did the Lord put before the people (1:18-20,27-28)?

    a. the wise thing the people could do _____

    _____

    _____

    how the Lord would respond _____

    _____

    _____

    _____

    b. the foolish course the people could take

    _____

    _____

26

how the Lord would respond _____

_____

_____

_____

Purge . . . dross (1:25). Gold or silver ore is melted in fire to remove its impurities, its dross.

5. The Lord planned to purge the dross from His people by turning His hand against them (1:25). What was His purpose in doing this (1:26-28)?

_____

_____

_____

_____

6. What do your observations from chapter 1 tell you about God's character and desires?

_____

_____

_____

_____

_____

For Thought and Discussion: a. Does the Lord ever turn His hand against you to purge your dross? If so, is this a good or a bad thing? Why?

b. How should you respond when you feel God is purging you?

For Thought and Discussion: Why doesn't the Lord just destroy rebels? What does 1:18-20 tell you about Him?

Study Skill—Summarizing the Passage
You will remember more of what you study if you summarize the main teaching of each passage. Consider these questions:

What is the Lord talking about in this passage?

What does this have to do with His overall message in the book?

Why does He say this here? (In this case, why does He begin the book with this prophecy?)

Optional Application:

Consider God's command in 1:17. In what ways, if any, do you "seek justice" and "encourage the oppressed"? How could you do so more than you are now? What would it cost you to actively seek justice, as well as simply avoiding committing injustice?

Optional Application: a. Meditate on the Lord's justice (1:19-20,24-28) and mercy (1:9,18). How have you experienced both of these in your life?

b. Thank the Lord for His justice and mercy toward you. How else could you respond?

7. How would you summarize the message of chapter 1?

_____

_____

_____

_____

Study Skill—Application

It can be helpful to plan an application in five steps:

1. Record the verse or passage that contains the truth you want to apply to your life. If the passage is short enough, consider copying it word for word, as an aid to memory.

2. State the truth of the passage that impresses you. For instance: *"The Lord hated Judah's worship because the people's professed love of God was false—it didn't move the worshipers to treat others with justice and compassion (1:10-17)."*

3. Tell how you fall short in relation to this truth. (Ask God to enable you to see yourself clearly.) For example: *"I don't personally cheat anyone, but I don't spend much time seeking justice and encouraging the oppressed either. I'm not even sure I know what that means. I don't know any vulnerable people like widows or orphans—at least, I haven't thought about whether I do."*

4. State precisely what you plan to do about having your life changed in this area. (Ask God what, if anything, you can do. Don't forget that transformation depends on His will, power, and timing, not on yours. Diligent prayer should always be part of your application.) For instance: *"First, I'm going to pray daily this week to learn who the 'oppressed' are in my community. I don't want to run off championing a cause where the Lord hasn't sent me. I'm going to discuss this with my small group to see if they have any ideas. It occurs to me that Marsha across the street isn't a widow, but she is divorced and her*

(continued on page 29)

28

(continued from page 28)

children are effectively 'fatherless.' I wonder how well they are managing? I think my wife and I should drop by with some brownies and find out if Marsha and her family need anything."

5. Plan a way to remind yourself to do what you have decided, such as putting a note on your refrigerator or in your office, or asking a friend or relative to remind you.⁵

8. Reread your answers to questions 1-7, and read the optional questions in the margins. Then, describe some ways in which you think 1:1-31 applies to Christians in general and you in particular.

_____

_____

_____

_____

_____

_____

_____

_____

_____

_____

9. What truth from 1:1-31 would you like to apply to your life this week?

_____

_____

_____

_____

Optional Application: Are you God's child and part of God's people? If so, how can you take 1:2-3 to heart this week in your prayer, thoughts, and actions?

Optional Application: Take time to "reason" with the Lord as described in 1:18-20. What would it mean for you to be "willing and obedient" (1:19)?

10. How do you fall short or want to grow in this area?

_____

_____

_____

_____

_____

_____

11. What steps can you take toward accomplishing this, by God's grace?

_____

_____

_____

_____

_____

_____

12. How can you remind yourself to do this?

_____

_____

_____

_____

13. If you have any questions about 1:1-31 or this lesson, write them here.

_____

_____

_____

_____

For the group

Worship.

Warm-up. Ask the group, "This week, have you behaved more like a rebellious or a willing and obedient child of God? How have you done this?"

Read aloud. It's always a good idea to read the passage before you discuss it. Someone might be present who hasn't prepared the lesson, and many people will appreciate having their memories refreshed. Ask someone (or a series of people) to read 1:1-31 with the tone of voice that Isaiah might have used when he proclaimed these words in Jerusalem. Recall that the Lord originally gave these prophecies to be announced aloud.

Summary. Before you plunge into the details of a passage, it's often helpful to summarize what the passage as a whole is about. What is the Lord saying in 1:1-31? Even though you have prepared the lesson ahead of time, you may not be able to summarize the chapter as well now as you will after discussing it. Still, this initial summary will start the group thinking. Just ask one or two people to give one-sentence summaries for now.

Questions. This study guide includes many notes on the text to help you understand Isaiah's message. Don't let them get in the way of your discussion, but do give group members a chance to ask questions about verses they don't understand. The sources on pages 213-216 may answer some questions.

Questions 1 through 5 of this lesson each touch on one of Isaiah's themes. They are:

1. What is the relationship between the Lord and Judah?
2. How has Judah sinned?
3. What are the consequences of sin?
4. What choice is the Lord offering Judah?
5. What is the Lord's purpose in judging Judah?

From these five themes you should be able to pull out three conclusions (questions 6-8):

6. What is the character of Isaiah's God?

31

Optional Application: Meditate on one or more of the Lord's titles. How does He reveal this side of Himself to you?

7. What is Isaiah's overall message?

8. How do God's character and Isaiah's message apply to us—specifically you—today?

Plan to spend about half of your time interpreting the passage and half considering applications. The optional questions suggest some ways of applying the passage, but don't feel limited by them.

Some people are used to talking about Scripture in Bible study groups but are not used to stating what they are going to do about it. A command like "Seek justice, encourage the oppressed" (1:17) has partisan political connotations that obscure its meaning and may hinder us from acting. Encourage your group to put what God says into practice.

On the other hand, some people are accustomed to scanning a passage for something applicable but are unpracticed at sorting out what the whole passage means. Help your group to see clearly what God was saying to Judah and only then to draw analogies to what He is saying to you. Good interpretation is essential for good application, but interpretation without application is pointless. Study Skills for interpreting and applying Isaiah are sprinkled through this study guide.

Note: *Don't* feel you must discuss every question in the lesson. The numbered questions are often just observations from the passage; the optional questions are often better meat for discussion. You can fruitfully spend a whole meeting on just one or two questions if you are thinking deeply and getting specific about application. There are more questions in the margins than you can possibly cover so that you can choose whatever interests your group. If you like, assign someone to look up cross-references for a question ahead of time.

The Names of God

The names Isaiah uses for God are never accidental; each has a specific meaning. As you study this book, be alert for these and other names:

1. **God.** *El* or *Elohim* in Hebrew. This is His status. Isaiah usually speaks of "our God" (1:10) or "the God of Jacob" (2:3) to distinguish Him from the "gods" of other nations.

(continued on page 33)

32

(continued from page 32)

2. **The LORD.** This is His personal name, rendered "Jehovah" or "Yahweh" in some versions (1:2,4). The Hebrew is *YHWH*, since Hebrew writing lacked vowels in Old Testament times. The Jews came to consider God's name too holy to be spoken, and so they began to say *Adonai*, "Lord," instead of *YHWH*.

YHWH is the name God gave when He delivered Israel from slavery and entered into an intimate covenant relationship with the nation. *YHWH* means "I AM" (Exodus 3:13-15, John 8:58-59). The Hebrew verb "to be" means not just "I exist," but "I am actively present." (Compare the name "Immanuel" in Isaiah 8:8,10.) *YHWH* is intimately, faithfully, dependably present. He "desires the full trust of his people."[6]

3. **The Lord.** The Hebrew *Adon* or *Adonai* (1:24, 6:1) means "Sovereign," "Master," "Ruler," "Lord."

4. **The LORD Almighty.** "The LORD of Hosts" (1:9) in other versions. This means YHWH "who is sovereign over all the 'hosts' (powers) in heaven and on earth, especially over the 'hosts' (armies) of Israel."[7]

5. **The Mighty One of Israel.** Again, this stresses God's power and sovereignty over, and on behalf of, Israel. He is Israel's Judge and Mighty Deliverer. The triple title in 1:24 is strong.

6. **The Holy One of Israel.** This title (1:4) "occurs 26 times in Isaiah and only 6 times elsewhere in the Old Testament."[8] It stresses God's holiness—His utter otherness from what is human, mortal, and earthly, and His perfect moral purity.[9]

---

1. Roland de Vaux, *Ancient Israel: Volume 1: Social Institutions* (New York: McGraw-Hill Book Company, 1965), pages 39-40.
2. The word *Israel* can be confusing in Isaiah. In some places it is the name of *the patriarch Jacob*, whom God renamed Israel (Genesis 32:28). More often, it is the name of *the nation of twelve tribes* with whom God made His covenant; the chosen people were named Israel after their common ancestor, Jacob. However, when Solomon's kingdom split, Israel became the name of *the northern nation* that was destroyed in Isaiah's day. That nation was also called Ephraim; its capital was Samaria.

Isaiah's primary audience is Judah (the southern nation) and its capital Jerusalem. Sometimes he speaks of Judah as part of "Israel" the chosen people, and sometimes he speaks of Judah as one nation and Israel as another. When the distinction is important, we will try to make it clear which "Israel" is meant in a question or verse, but often we will leave the issue aside.

3. Madeleine S. and J. Lane Miller, *Harper's Encyclopedia of Bible Life* (San Francisco: Harper and Row, 1978), page 184; *NIV Study Bible*, page 1018.

4. *NIV Study Bible*, page 1019.

5. This "Five-point Application" is based on the method in *The 2:7 Series*, Course 4 (Colorado Springs: NavPress, 1979), pages 50-51.

6. *NIV Study Bible*, page 91.

7. *NIV Study Bible*, page xii.

8. *NIV Study Bible*, page 1018.

9. J. A. Motyer, "The Names of God," *Eerdmans' Handbook to the Bible*, edited by David and Pat Alexander (Grand Rapids, Michigan: William B. Eerdmans Publishing Company, 1973), pages 157-158.

ISAIAH 2:1-4:6

Pride

In chapters 2 through 4, Isaiah speaks about "the day of the LORD." Judah knows it will be the day when the Lord triumphs over His enemies and restores justice to the whole world. Surely then (Judah reasons) that day will be glory and victory for us, God's chosen people! Well (the Lord warns in these oracles), that depends on Judah's attitude.

Read 2:1-4:6 before beginning the questions. Look for the two sides of the day of the Lord—joyful and terrifying. Notice how the subtitles in this lesson break the passage into four parts. The outline on page 18 may also be helpful to you.

The joy of God's justice (2:1-5)

For Judah during the reign of Jotham, it is shocking that "many peoples" (2:3), not just the chosen nation of Israel, will be able to go to the Lord for instruction and revelation of Himself. This theme of God's welcome to the nations recurs in Isaiah's book.

The last days (2:2). These began with Christ's first coming (Acts 2:17, Hebrews 1:2) and will be completed at His second coming.[1] The prophecies of the last days have begun to be fulfilled, but their final fulfillment will be just before Christ's return.

Optional Application: How can you obey 2:5 during the coming week? Take some time to meditate on this verse, and write down any specific practical steps that you think of. (See 1 John 1:5-10.) Write in a separate notebook or in questions 13 and 14.

For Further Study: Examine other passages that compare the Lord to light, such as Isaiah 60:1-2, 19-20; Psalm 27:1; John 1:1-9; 1 John 1:5-7. What happens to us when we walk in the light of the Lord (2 Corinthians 3:18)?

Mountain of the LORD's temple (2:2). Jerusalem itself was on the peak of Mount Zion, and the Temple was at the city's highest point.

Law (2:3). *Torah* in Hebrew. This includes laws in the sense of rules of conduct, as well as instruction, guidance, teaching, and revelation. See Jeremiah 31:31-34; Romans 8:1-2; James 1:22-25.

1. What will God do for many peoples when they come to Him (2:3-4)?

_____

_____

_____

_____

2. What will be the result when all people acknowledge the Lord as their Teacher and rightful Judge (2:4)?

_____

_____

_____

_____

3. In 2:5, Isaiah tells how we should act in the present because of this future hope. What does it mean to "walk in the light of the LORD"? (*Optional:* See John 3:19-21, 8:12. You might ask God to help you understand this concept.)

_____

_____

_____

_____

_____

4. Since Christ first came, 2:2-5 has begun to be fulfilled. Why must we be walking in the light

36

of the Lord (2:5) in order for the nations to stream to Him (2:2-4)?

_____

_____

_____

_____

_____

For Thought and Discussion: What is pride?

For Thought and Discussion: What will men do when the Lord humiliates them (2:10,17-20)?

The dread of God's justice (2:6-22)

The day when the Lord's authority is exalted will be good news from one point of view (2:2-5), but 2:6-22 looks at that day from another point of view. Notice the repeated verses in this passage.

Majesty (2:10,19,21) and *pride* (2:11,12,17). Literally, "loftiness" as in NASB and KJV. The same Hebrew words are used for an attribute of God and a sin of man.

5. Why is loftiness (exaltation, highness) acceptable for God but wrong and foolish for man (2:21-22)?

_____

_____

_____

_____

_____

Cedars . . . oaks . . . mountains . . . hills . . . tower . . . wall . . . ship . . . vessel (2:13-16). Even natural and man-made things that impress humans will be leveled before the Lord when He alone is exalted.

37

For Further Study:
a. Malachi 4:1-6 is parallel to Isaiah 2:1-22. Both passages describe what will happen when the Lord appears. Why does the sun of righteousness consume the wicked but heal the faithful?
    b. How does Malachi 4:1-6 help you understand Isaiah 2:5?

For Further Study:
For New Testament parallels to Isaiah 2:6-22, see Matthew 5:3,5; Mark 10:41-45; Luke 14:7-11; 1 Peter 5:5-7.

For Thought and Discussion: Why are idols, magic, wealth, and armaments signs of pride (2:6-9)?

6. How do men show their pride and arrogance, according to 2:6-8,15-16? (List as many ways as you can.)

_____

_____

_____

_____

_____

_____

7. What will make men abandon their pride (2:10,19,21)?

_____

_____

_____

8. Consider each of the things in which Judah found pride and security (2:6-8). Do you take pride in anything besides God? If so, what are you proud about, and how do you show it?

_____

_____

_____

_____

_____

False supports lost (3:1-4:1)

In chapter 2, Isaiah seemed to be talking primarily about the end times (2:2), although in some sense his prophecy applied to his own generation of Jews

(2:6-9). Chapter 3 seems more directly addressed to Judah in the time of Jotham, but it has a message for every age.

Soothsayer . . . enchanter (3:2-3). "Prudent" and "orator" in KJV. Occult practitioners were forbidden sources of help (Deuteronomy 18:10-12). The other sources of help in Isaiah 3:2-3 were normally legitimate, but the Lord would remove them also.[2]

---

9. In chapter 3, the Lord portrays the way He will humble His people by taking away all sources of support. Write down as many lost supports as you can find in 3:1-7 and 3:16-4:1.

_____

_____

_____

_____

_____

_____

_____

10. What are some of your sources of support, besides the Lord?

_____

_____

_____

_____

_____

_____

Optional Application: What would happen to you if you lost your greatest sources of support, other than the Lord? Pray about this. Do you need to change any attitudes?

39

For Thought and Discussion:
a. Whom does God blame primarily for His people's depravity (3:13-15)?

b. Does this fact have any implications for the Church? If so, what are they? If not, why not?

For Thought and Discussion: Is there a lesson in 3:16-4:1 for modern women? If so, what might it be?

Study Skill—Prophetic Forms: the Lawsuit
The prophets sometimes conveyed the Lord's message in certain literary forms that people would recognize. One such form is the *lawsuit,* which portrays the Lord as a sovereign bringing suit against a subject for breaking a covenant/treaty. "The full lawsuit contains a summons, a charge, evidence, and a verdict, though these elements may sometimes be implied rather than explicit."[3]

In Isaiah 1:2, the Lord called heaven and earth as His witnesses. Now in 3:8-15 He uses the lawsuit form more fully. Notice the judge (3:13), the defendant (3:14), the accusation (3:8-9,12,14-15), and the verdict and sentence (3:10-11). Watch for the lawsuit form in later passages; Isaiah uses it frequently.

Women (3:16-4:1). In the Near East, a person's manner of walking showed her attitudes, and her clothing and ornaments displayed her station. Shaving the head bald (3:17,24) was a sign of mourning, and the rope belt, sackcloth clothing, and branding (3:24) were marks of a slave. In other words, war was going to reduce Judah's well-to-do women to childless, widowed, impoverished slaves—the lowest status possible in the Near East.[4]

True support restored (4:2-6)

After humiliation comes restoration. As he began this set of oracles in 2:1-5, so Isaiah ends it—with an oracle of hope. The very day[5] of Zion's desolation (4:1) will be the day of her restoration (4:2).

Branch (4:2). The Hebrew words for shoot or branch do not mean just a part of a tree or a little sprout of growth. Rather, a "branch" is an abundantly and freshly alive "growing thing."[6]

In Isaiah 11:1, 53:2; Jeremiah 23:5, 33:15; Zechariah 3:8, 6:12, the "Branch" is a title for the Messiah, the Savior King who would be descended from David. In Isaiah 4:2, however, the "Branch" may be the holy nation or the great work of salvation which will flourish when God brings it to fulfillment.[7] Compare John 15:5.

Optional Application: Meditate on the character the Lord reveals in 2:1-4:6, especially on His justice in 3:10-11 and His grace in 4:3-4. How might His character affect the way you act during the coming week? (You might discuss this with another person or with your group.)

11. Isaiah lists many things that will be true "in that day," in contrast to what he has described in 2:6-4:1.

    a. In contrast to the women in 3:16-23, "the Branch of the LORD will be beautiful and glorious" in that day (4:2). Who do you think the Branch is in this passage?

    _____

    _____

    b. Recall the sources of pride named in chapters 2 and 3. What will be the source of pride for those who survive God's judgment (4:2).

    _____

    _____

    _____

    c. According to 4:3, how will the survivors' moral character be different from the character described in 3:8-9?

    _____

    _____

    _____

    _____

    d. What will be the survivors' source of security (4:5-6), unlike the sources named in 2:6-8 and 3:1-7?

    _____

For Further Study: On the spirit of judgment and fire, see Malachi 4:1-6 and Luke 3:16-17.

41

For Thought and Discussion:
a. According to 4:2-6, do those who are saved earn their deliverance or receive it as a gift? How can you tell? (Does Isaiah agree with Ephesians 2:8-9?)
b. According to 4:3, only *holy* people will be able to live in the holy city of God. How does a person become holy (4:4)?

For Thought and Discussion: What is the purpose of judgment in the life of one who is saved (4:4)? How does this fact apply to you?

Optional Application: Telling someone about what you have learned can help you to remember and apply it. To whom could you tell the most significant things you learned from 2:1-4:6?

Cloud . . . fire . . . canopy . . . shelter (4:5-6). During the forty years when Israel wandered in the desert before entering the promised land, a cloud led and protected the people. It was a cloud of smoke to shade from the sun or storm during the day, and a cloud of fire to warm and ward off animals during the night. As it hovered overhead, it was like a canopy or a tent (tabernacle, shelter). The cloud was called the *shekinah*, the glory of the Lord, the outward manifestation of His presence. See Exodus 13:21-22, 40:34-38. Isaiah foresaw God again doing something like what He did at the Exodus.

Your response

12. In general, chapters 2-4 are about the effects of God's exaltation (2:2,11) and judgment (3:10-11, 4:2-4) on two kinds of people. How would you summarize what the Lord says in 2:1-4:6?

_____

_____

_____

_____

_____

13. What seems to be the most important insight you have gained from studying 2:1-4:6? Prayerfully review this lesson, and write down any ways that the Lord's words apply to you.

_____

_____

_____

_____

_____

14. Is there any action (including prayer) you plan to take in response to what the Lord has said? If so, what is it?

_____

_____

_____

_____

_____

_____

For Further Study:
Making an outline yourself is often more useful than reading someone else's. The outline on pages 18-20 is just one of many good possibilities. Try outlining 1:1-4:6 or 2:1-4:6 in as much detail as you find helpful.

Study Skill—Application

It can be hard to be "doers of the word, and not merely hearers" (James 1:22 NASB), but the key is to be actively relying on God. For instance, let's say your desired application for chapter 2 is "I need to be more humble." How can you accomplish that? Not overnight. Still, here are some beginning steps:

1. When you decide you can't achieve humility without God, you are on your way. Ask Him for the power and wisdom to become more humble. Ask repeatedly, daily. Listen for guidance.

2. Confess any ways you show pride: boasting, craving praise, hurting when criticized, criticizing yourself. Confess any sources of pride: appearance, possessions, intellect, accomplishments. Ask God to forgive you, and believe that you are forgiven (Psalm 32:1-5).

3. Look for circumstances that require humility—times when you succeed and times when you fail. If you find yourself feeling either proud or worthless, then humble yourself before God and repeat (1) and (2).

4. Using a concordance of the Bible (see page 215 of this guide), study many refer-

(continued on page 44)

(continued from page 43)
ences to pride and humility. Write down as
accurately as you can exactly what pride and
humility are. (Is humility the same as feeling
worthless?) List as many reasons as possible
for being humble.

15. List any questions you have about 2:1-4:6.

_____

_____

_____

_____

For the group

Worship.

Warm-up. Since the two themes of this lesson are
the day of the Lord and pride, you could ask as a
warm-up, "What is pride?" Don't expect deep
answers at this point; the question is meant only to
stimulate people's thinking. Tell the group to keep
the question in mind during your discussion.

Read aloud. You might prefer to read just
2:1-5,12-18; 4:1-6 to sense the changes in mood
from joy to wrath to joy.

Summary. After the above warm-up, if you ask,
"Overall, what is 2:1-4:6 about?" be prepared to be
told, "Pride." Ask for a slightly more thorough
response than this, but don't push for perfection.
The group will be able to do better after discussing
the passages.

God's Justice. Chapter 2 deals with the two sides of
God's justice. The pleasant side is the peace that
results when people acknowledge God as their
Teacher and Judge (2:1-5); the unpleasant side is
the uproar that results when they don't (2:6-22).
This fact, as well as what pride and humility are, are
the main points of questions 1-8.

Application. You can ask application questions at

any point in the discussion. Some possibilities are: "How does 2:5 apply to us? How should God's justice affect our actions? How can we make sure that the day of the Lord wil be a joyful day for us?" Try to help people to be as specific with their answers as possible.

Three things keep people from discussing specific applications in Bible study. One is time; you should try to allow about half of your discussion time for application. Another is shyness; people may be unwilling to reveal their private needs and weaknesses. If so, take time to build familiarity and trust among the group members. There are many good books on how to do this. You should not force anyone to bare his soul who would rather not.

A third reason why people are unspecific about application is ignorance; no one has ever explained to them how to apply Scripture. Your group can be a place for learning this skill and developing a desire to use it. In any given week, a person should aim to deal with one issue the Bible has illuminated in his or her life. He need not take on a new issue each week just because the Bible study has moved on, as long as he is still dealing with last week's issue. If a person is still persistently praying about something God raised in lesson one, the group should encourage him or her.

The group can be a great help in application if everyone pursues a right attitude. You can discuss possible ways of applying 2:1-4:6 this week, and at the beginning of your next meeting you can discuss any successes and difficulties you encountered. At that time, you can encourage each other to persevere when God doesn't change you overnight or when you fail to do what you planned. You can also pray for each other between meetings.

False and true supports. Chapter 3 is covered at lightning speed. If necessary, you can slow down and see that everyone understands what is going on in each paragraph. That will probably take an extra meeting.

It is often helpful to ask quick questions about the background material, such as the Study Skill or the information about the women on page 40. However, don't let the background material distract you from following the passage's message.

If you are covering lesson three in one meeting, be sure to focus on the list of false supports in 3:1-4:1, so that you can contrast them with the true sources of pride and security in 4:2-6. You might want to name modern equivalents of the false supports or ask each group member to think of one source of pride or security he has besides the Lord. See the suggestions for application above.

Summarize. After discussing the contrasts in question 11, the group should be able to summarize the Lord's message in 2:1-4:6. Ask one or two people to do this, and one or two to summarize how the passages apply to you.

Wrap-up. If you intend to discuss your progress on application when you next meet, ask the group to be prepared to do this. A simple method would be to say, "We've talked about how to apply to ourselves what Isaiah says. Can everyone come next week prepared to share what happened when you tried to do this? I think we'd all learn a lot from hearing how everybody else went about letting God change his or her life."

Worship. Praise God for whatever traits most strike you in 2:1-4:6—majesty, justice, mercy, etc. Isaiah is an ideal book for focusing on God's character.

A somewhat contrived exercise for groups who aren't used to praising God together would be to take turns praying one sentence of praise, such as, "O God, you have the right to judge between the nations" or "O Lord, you are higher than anyone else." Doing this in a group for the first time can help anyone feel humble! However, if you suspect that the group will feel self-conscious doing this, you might just take a few minutes for silent praise and prayer.

1. *The NIV Study Bible*, page 1020; Leupold, volume 1, page 75.
2. *The NIV Study Bible*, page 1021; Leupold, volume 1, pages 89-90.
3. Fee and Stuart, page 150.
4. *The NIV Study Bible*, page 1022.
5. Most scholars think the day of the Lord is not a literal 24-hour day, but that is debated.
6. Leupold, volume 1, page 102.
7. Leupold, volume 1, page 102; *The NIV Study Bible*, page 1023.

ISAIAH 5:1-6:13

The Prophet Sent

If you are tired of reading about woe and judgment, just imagine how weary Isaiah must have gotten proclaiming judgment to a nation that paid no attention! By the end of chapter 5 you should have a good idea of why God was angry with Judah, so you should be able to understand the strange mission God gave to Isaiah.

Read 5:1-6:13.

The vineyard (5:1-7)

Isaiah was a master of many literary forms which he adapted to his purpose. This time he uses the rhythm of a Hebrew love song and the technique of a parable to make his point.

1. What is the message of the parable in 5:1-7?

_____

_____

_____

_____

_____

_____

For Thought and Discussion: How does God feel about Israel, according to 5:1-7?

47

For Further Study:
Why is the conse-
quence of each sin in
5:8-30 appropriate?
(For instance, why
does 5:9-10 fit 5:8?)

2. How does 5:1-7 portray God's character?

_____

_____

_____

_____

_____

Woes and judgments (5:8-30)

Study Skill—Prophetic Forms: the Woe

You saw a covenant lawsuit in chapter 3 and a parable song in 5:1-7. In 5:8-30, Isaiah uses another prophetic form, the woe. "'Woe' was the word ancient Israelites cried out when facing disaster or death, or when they mourned at a funeral."[1] It is a wail of sorrow, not of hostility.

A woe oracle usually contains three elements: an announcement of distress ("woe"), the reason for distress (the injustices that the people were committing), and a prediction of disaster.[2] Isaiah 5:8-30 contains six woes.

House to house (5:8). "Land in Israel could only be leased, never sold, because parcels had been permanently assigned to individual families"[3] (Numbers 27:7-11, 1 Kings 21:1-3). The land belonged to the Lord; the people were His tenants (Leviticus 25:23). His Law declared that leased land must revert to its original owners every fifty years (Leviticus 25:8-24). However, in Isaiah's time rich men were buying peasants' land and ignoring the fifty-year limit.

Bath . . . ephah (5:10). A bath was about six gallons, a homer was about six bushels, and an ephah was about half a bushel. A ten-acre vineyard and a homer of seed should have produced many times that much wine and grain.

48

Deuteronomy 28:38-39 promised that national sin would lead to poor crops.

Cords . . . ropes (5:18). These people do not fall reluctantly into sin; they drag heavy loads of it eagerly. They scoff at Isaiah's promise that God's retribution will be as swift as their stampede into sin.

A banner (5:26). A banner (standard, signal, ensign) was often planted on a hill as a signal for gathering troops.[4]

For Thought and Discussion: What does 5:8-30 tell you about what God loves and hates?

3. Explain the meaning of each of the six sins the Lord condemns in 5:8-30.

5:8

5:11-12

5:18-19

5:20

5:21

5:22-23

---

4. Ask the Lord if you have tendencies toward any sins like those you listed in question 3. Does 5:8-30 have any implications for your life? If so what are they?

_____

_____

_____

_____

_____

_____

_____

Isaiah's commission (6:1-13)

King Uzziah died in 740 BC. Isaiah probably delivered the oracles of 1:1-5:30 after this vision of God, but he describes the vision here as a climax and justification of his offensive pronouncements.[5]

5. Describe what Isaiah saw and heard (6:1-4), and tell what each fact you note tells you about God.

what Isaiah saw and heard	what it tells about God
"the Lord," "the LORD Almighty"	*He is sovereign over all, all powerful, the God who is present.*

Optional Application: Meditate on the person of God as He reveals Himself in 5:1-6:4. Does looking at Him make you see yourself as Isaiah saw himself (6:5)? Why or why not?

For Thought and Discussion: Why do you think seraphs cover their faces and feet in the Lord's presence?

For Thought and Discussion: Why must God's messengers have clean lips?

Optional Application: How clean are your lips? Pray about this.

6. In 5:8-30, Isaiah mourned for his nation. Why does he mourn for himself in the same way when he sees the Lord (6:5)?

_____

_____

_____

_____

_____

Seraphs (6:2,6). These angelic beings are named nowhere else in Scripture, although they resemble the "living creatures" of Revelation 4:6-9, which also have six wings. The Hebrew root of *seraph* means "burn."[6]

Atoned for (6:7). "Forgiven" in NASB; "purged" in KJV. To atone is literally "to cover." It means to pay the price of a sin, to make satisfaction for it. The system of burnt sacrifices was instituted to impress this idea of atonement on Israel. The price of sin was death, but animals symbolically paid that price for the people. Later, God would show that it had always been God the Son who had paid the death penalty to atone for man's sin, but for now the burning coals on the altar represented God's provision for man's sin.[7]

7. What are "unclean lips" (6:5)? (*Optional:* See 59:3-5,14-15.)

_____

_____

_____

_____

_____

8. a. What did the seraph's act in 6:6-7 signify?

_____

52

_____

_____

_____

b. In light of 6:5, why was this act necessary
   before God could give Isaiah a prophetic
   mission?

_____

_____

_____

_____

9. Verses 9-10 are not a malicious curse. The Lord
   knows how the people will respond to Isaiah's
   warning, and He pronounces the inevitable
   consequences. What is the necessary result of
   refusing to listen to God? (*Optional:* See Ephesians 4:18.)

_____

_____

_____

_____

_____

10. Think about Isaiah's mission (6:9-13). Why
    would God send someone with a message that
    was only going to make the people more
    stubborn?

_____

_____

_____

_____

_____

For Further Study:
Jesus quoted Isaiah
6:9-10 in Matthew
13:9-17. Why did
Jesus speak plainly to
His disciples but ob-
scurely to the crowd?
How should Jesus'
words move us to
act?

For Further Study:
Why does God give
ears to some of us
deaf sinners but
hardens others
(Isaiah 6:9-10)? Paul
wrestled with why
God had deafened so
many of his fellow
Jews. Romans 9-11 is
his attempt at an
explanation. You
might look at Romans
1:18-21; 9:14-24;
11:1-16,25-32. There
are also books on this
subject.

Optional Application: Think about the character qualities Isaiah showed before the Lord (6:5,8). Consider his willingness to carry out such a grim and seemingly point-less mission. How could you respond to God similarly?

For Thought and Discussion: Summarize your impressions of God's character from 6:1-13.

11. a. How did Isaiah feel about his mission (6:11)?

_____

_____

_____

_____

b. What does his willingness to bear the message of 6:9-10 tell you about him?

_____

_____

_____

_____

_____

12. God told Isaiah ahead of time that the people would ignore him and so be decimated and dec-imated again. This was all part of God's plan. But what hope did He leave Isaiah (6:13)? Explain in your own words.

_____

_____

_____

_____

13. Go back over the questions in this lesson and what you have written. What one aspect of 5:1-6:13 would you like to take to heart during the coming week?

_____

_____

_____

_____

14. How would you like this truth to affect your life?

_____

_____

_____

_____

_____

15. What steps can you take toward accomplishing this by God's grace?

_____

_____

_____

_____

_____

16. Write down any questions you have about 5:1-6:13.

_____

_____

_____

_____

_____

Optional Application: Sometimes confession and worship are the most appropriate responses to a passage. Consider taking fifteen full minutes just for this.

For Further Study: Add 5:1-6:13 to your outline of Isaiah. In your titles for 1:1-6:13 and your labels for each passage, try to show how 1:1-6:13 fits together as a unit. What is the whole section about, and how does each passage fit?

For the group

Worship.

Warm-up. Ask, "Remember the last time you felt strongly convicted of sin. How did you feel? What led you to feel convicted?" You don't have to discuss this question, just take a minute or two of silence to let everyone remember. This time can prepare for your discussion of 6:5.

This would be a good time to discuss how the past week's applications went, if you plan to do this. As people share problems with scheduling time for prayer, remembering, coming up with something specific to pray or do, or feeling guilty, let the group encourage each other and suggest solutions. Watch for tendencies to boast, complain, or condemn.

Read aloud. You might take turns reading the parable, each of the six woes, and 6:1-13. Try to let the emotions of these passages touch you.

Summarize. Ask someone to explain briefly what chapters 5 and 6 are each about. You might have someone remind the group of what chapters 1-4 said, and how 5:1-6:13 is connected to what comes before.

Questions. This lesson is fairly straightforward. Its theme is "What was Isaiah's mission?" and it also reveals much about the characters of God and a righteous man. Question 10 is perhaps the most difficult and crucial question. It should not be speculative, but rather a challenge to understand God's character and plan. The boxes entitled, "Old Testament Prophets" (pages 57-58, 68, and 90) may help you understand Isaiah's mission.

You won't be able to discuss all the questions in this lesson in one meeting. Choose a few, and try to delve deeply. If passages like 6:9-10 mystify you, consider borrowing a commentary on Isaiah.

Rephrasing. In even the best Bible study guide, you will sometimes find a question unclear. However, you can usually reduce any question to one of three basic questions: What does this passage tell us about God—who He is and what He does? What does it tell us about man (or woman)? What does it tell us a Christian should do? The question will normally be asking you either to *observe* what the passage says, *interpret* what it means, or *apply* it to yourselves.

These guidelines will also help you to make the discussion more interesting for the group. For instance, instead of always asking, "What did you get for number 1?" you can ask, "What does 5:1-7 *say* about Israel?" "What did you learn about Israel from 5:1-7?" "How does 5:1-7 reveal God's character?" "Could God say about us what He said about

Israel? Why or why not?" or any of a dozen similar questions.

Application. Allow time for each person to share how he or she plans to respond to or act on something from 5:1-6:13. Some people may prefer not to share, and others may want to continue praying and thinking about something from lesson three. Respect everyone's wishes, but also draw out at least one or two ways that someone might apply 5:1-6:13. Those ways will give the group models to adapt for future applications.

Summarize. As in lesson three, summarize the discussion of both the passage's meaning and its application. This will help people to focus their ideas and to remember what has been said.

Worship. Many songs use the words and ideas of Isaiah 6 for worship. You might sing one together, or take time for silent meditation on the majesty those verses depict.

Old Testament Prophets, part one

The Hebrew word, "prophet" (*nabi*) comes from the verb "to call" (*nabu*). It indicates that the prophet was uniquely called to be intimate with the Lord and to speak for Him. A related word is "seer," one who "sees" the plans and judgments of the Lord.

There had been prophets in Israel ever since the Lord gave Moses the Law on Mount Sinai. Moses was the first prophet of the Law, and just before his death he promised that Israel would have a series of prophets after him (Deuteronomy 18:14-22). The prophets' main job "was to *speak* for God to their own contemporaries."[8] They were His messengers, His ambassadors.

A prophet's task was not so much to predict the future as to contradict the present. "Israel, you think you are doing fine, but in fact you are in sin and ripe for judgment." Or, "You think things are bleak, but fear not: God is at work." The prophet told forth the Lord's assessment of the current situation and foretold how the Lord planned to respond.

(continued on page 58)

(continued from page 57)

The prophets were not radical social and religious thinkers transforming Israel's faith. Rather, from Moses through John the Baptist, they measured justice and religion against the standard of the covenant agreement.

(continued on page 68)

1. Fee and Stuart, page 160.
2. Fee and Stuart, page 160.
3. *The NIV Study Bible,* page 1024.
4. *The NIV Study Bible,* page 1025.
5. Kidner, page 595.
6. *The NIV Study Bible,* page 1025.
7. William Owen Carver, "Atonement," *The International Standard Bible Encyclopaedia,* volume 1, edited by James Orr, pages 321-324.
8. Fee and Stuart, page 150.

ISAIAH 7:1-8:22

Facing Danger

Chapters 7 through 12 are the second section of Isaiah's book. His commission in chapter 6 took place in 740 BC, and chapter 7 picks up again in about 735 BC.

Ahaz, Uzziah's grandson, is now king. Isaiah is known to be a prophet; he freely voices his views to Ahaz despite hostility from the rest of the royal counselors. The political situation is precarious: King Rezin of Aram (Syria) and King Pekah of Israel (Ephraim) have allied against Assyria. They are threatening to invade Judah unless Ahaz joins them. Ahaz's counselors are urging him to seek Assyria's help against Rezin and Pekah, but Isaiah foresees disaster on that road. Chapters 7-12 recount Isaiah's attempt to dissuade Ahaz and also include the Lord's encouragement in this situation.

Have you ever been in an impossible situation, where you wish you could just hide and make it go away? Ahaz and Isaiah knew that one wrong move could plunge the nation into bloody war, but Isaiah saw the Lord's hand on the present and the future.

Read 7:1-8:22. The subtitles in this lesson and the outline on page 18 may help you to orient yourself.

Immanuel (7:1-25)

Head (7:8-9). The capitals of Aram and Ephraim are only Damascus and Samaria. The rulers of those

For Thought and Discussion: Isaiah's name means "The LORD is salvation." Why did Ahaz need to be reminded of this?

For Thought and Discussion: In Luke 11:14-16,29-32, Jesus is angry at people who ask for a sign to prove He is from God, immediately after He has just healed a mute man. Why was it wrong for those people to ask Jesus for a sign, and wrong for Ahaz not to ask?

cities are only Rezin and Pekah. Those men are trivial compared to Judah's Head, the Lord.

1. Reread 7:1-11. How does God want Ahaz to respond to the threat of invasion?

   a. 7:4,9 _____

   _____

   _____

   _____

   b. 7:11 _____

   _____

Isaiah said (7:13). The Hebrew says "*he* said" (KJV, NASB), but the context suggests that Isaiah is giving God's retort to Ahaz.

2. In 7:10-13, Ahaz's disobedience makes God angry. What choices and attitudes might have moved Ahaz to refuse God's invitation?

   _____

   _____

   _____

   _____

Virgin (7:14). The Hebrew word *almah* means "maiden," "unmarried woman." By implication in Hebrew culture, such a woman is a virgin.[1]

The Lord allowed Ahaz to name any sign he wanted, but when he refused, the Lord gave a sign of His choosing (7:13-16). Commentators agree that the sign applies in its fullest sense to Christ. Some[2] feel that it applies to Christ alone and was not really a sign for Ahaz. Others[3] feel it had a first fulfillment in Isaiah's day and a

60

second at Christ's birth. The immediate fulfill-ment may have been that a virgin in the palace was soon to be married and have a son. When the boy reached the age of accountability, about twelve or thirteen years old, he was eating the diet of a herdsman because an invasion had made agriculture impossible (7:15). But even before then, Aram and Israel were destroyed (7:16).

In fact, the prophecies in 7:8,15-17 were definitely fulfilled in this sense. Within sixty-five years, or by 670 BC (7:8), Israel had been depopulated of the chosen people and repopu-lated with pagans from other countries. Within thirteen years, or by 721 BC (7:15-17), Israel was devastated and agriculture in Judah was dis-rupted by the Assyrian invasion.

---

3. Are God's words to Ahaz (7:4,9,11,13) relevant to you in any ways? If so, how?

_____

_____

_____

_____

4. In Matthew 1:18-25 the Lord revealed that the sign He gave to Ahaz's generation had a second fulfillment—the virgin birth of Jesus. "Imman-uel" means "God with us." In the time of Ahaz, God was with His people to protect them from enemies (7:7-8, 8:9-10). How is Jesus a still greater fulfillment of the sign-name, "God with us"?

_____

_____

_____

_____

_____

Optional Application: a. Can you identify with Ahaz's fears and atti-tudes? If so, how?

b. In what current circumstances do you need to "stand firm in your faith" (7:9)?

For Thought and Discussion: Read 7:13-25. What do you learn about God's character and methods from the way he dealt with Ahaz?

For Further Study: Study more about standing firm (Isaiah 7:9) in Galatians 5:1, Ephesians 6:10-18, and 1 Peter 5:8-9. How is it possible for Christians to stand firm?

Optional Application: Con-sider meditating on 7:9b or 7:14.

Optional Application: How is Immanuel's presence with you an encour-agement in your situation?

For Thought and Discussion: a. What is the Lord's point in 8:6-8? (Who do the waters of Jerusalem and the floodwaters of Assyria signify?)

b. Judah had reason to fear Assyria, but why did Assyria have reason to fear (8:9-10)?

Study Skill—Poetic Imagery

Isaiah uses some striking images to describe the Assyrian invasion. He says that the soldiers will be like the painful flies that infest the Nile in Egypt, and like bees from Assyria (7:18-19). It was a great insult to forcibly shave a man, and Isaiah says that what the Assyrian king will do will be just as humiliating (7:20). In 8:6-8, Isaiah uses flowing water as an image to make his point. Watch for other figurative, pictorial language in Isaiah's prophecies—images of light and darkness, sun and storm, trees, axes, and clothing.

God uses Assyria (8:1-10)

Witnesses (8:2). Isaiah 8:1-2 describes a legal transaction. Uriah and Zechariah may be witnessing Isaiah's marriage to "the prophetess" (8:3), or witnessing that Isaiah prophesied the name of his son before Assyria's invasion. Isaiah gave his first son a symbolic name—*Shear-Jashub* means "a remant will return" (7:3, 10:21-22); Immanuel's name means "God is with us"; and now Isaiah gives his second son a name meaning "quick to the plunder, swift to the spoil" (8:3). The name prophesies that Assyria will plunder Israel and Judah.

In 8:4, the Lord promises that before the new baby is two or three years old, Assyria will plunder Aram and Israel. The baby was probably born in 733/732 BC, and by 731/730 the Assyrian army had indeed begun to despoil Israel and Aram.

The waters of Shiloah (8:6). Probably part of Jerusalem's water supply.[4]

The River (8:7). The Euphrates River in Assyria. The Lord is punning in 8:6-8. Because the people have rejected the gentle waters of Jerusalem, they will get the floodwaters of Assyria.

Fear God (8:11-22)

Conspiracy (8:12). God doesn't specify which of the many intrigues in Jerusalem He means. There were pro-Assyrian, pro-Egyptian, anti-Ahaz, and anti-Isaiah factions. Aram and Ephraim were allied, and Isaiah may have been accused of being a conspirator. God's counsel applies to all of these.

---

5. How does God want Isaiah to respond to intrigues, the danger of invasion, and accusations from his countrymen (8:11-13)?

_____

_____

_____

_____

6. a. What does it mean to "fear" and "dread" the Lord in a good sense (8:13)?

_____

_____

_____

_____

_____

b. Why is this important for us to do? (*Optional:* See Proverbs 1:7, Luke 12:4-12.)

_____

_____

_____

_____

_____

For Thought and Discussion:
a. Why must the Lord be our fear before He can be our sanctuary (8:13-14)?
b. How can we both fear and love God?

Optional Application: Do you fear the Lord in a good sense (8:13)? If so, how do you show it? If not how can you develop a healthy fear of God?

For Thought and Discussion: What kind of fear of God is not good to have?

63

Optional Application: How is the Lord like a rock in your life?

For Further Study:
a. In a concordance, find other references to the Lord as a Rock, such as Isaiah 28:16.
    b. Look at how Isaiah 8:14 is applied to Christ in Romans 9:33 and 1 Peter 2:6-8.

Optional Application: a. How do people today deal with the uncertainties of the future?
    b. How do you deal with uncertainties? Does 8:16-20 have any lessons you can take to heart? If so, ask the Lord to instill them in you.

For Thought and Discussion: What do light and darkness symbolize in 8:19-22?

7. a. The Lord is often compared to a rock in the Old Testament. How is He like a rock for those who fear *Him* (Isaiah 8:14, 28:16; Psalm 62:1-2)?

_____

_____

_____

_____

b. How is He like a rock for those who fear *people and circumstances* (8:14)?

_____

_____

_____

_____

Testimony . . . law (8:16,20). Probably Isaiah's teaching about the Lord and his prophecies about the Assyrian invasion. He seals it like a legal document to be held by his disciples as future proof that the Lord planned and brought about the events. God was going to prove Isaiah a true prophet, and the prophecy was going to prove God sovereign over history. *Law* can also refer to the books of Moses, or to "teaching, instruction," revelation in general.[5]

I . . . children (8:18). In 8:17-20, Isaiah was probably speaking of himself as "I" and his sons or disciples as his "children." However, he was also speaking prophetically of what Christ would say (Hebrews 2:13).[6]

8. a. How were people in Jerusalem dealing with uncertainties about the future (8:19)?

_____

_____

64

b. How was Isaiah determined to deal with uncertainty (8:16-17,20)?

_____

_____

_____

_____

_____

9. When invasion brings disaster, the prophet and his disciples are signs from the Lord to the faithless nation (8:18). How can Christians be signs from the Lord?

_____

_____

_____

_____

_____

10. Does 7:1-8:22 offer any guidance for Christians facing fearful circumstances? If so, summarize the guidance it offers.

_____

_____

_____

_____

_____

Your response

11. Describe one insight from 7:1-8:22 that you would like to apply to your life.

_____

_____

_____

For Thought and Discussion: How does 8:18 apply to Christ and the Church (Hebrews 2:11-15)? How does it apply to you?

For Thought and Discussion: What is the Lord's overall point in 8:1-22?

Optional Application: Meditate on 7:9, 8:12-14, or some other verses, and make a list of the implications the verses have for your life.

65

Optional Application: Are you currently faced with any threats, accusations, factions, or conspiracies? How does 8:11-13,19-20 encourage you to respond? Try planning some specific course of action that includes prayer.

For Thought and Discussion: What themes does 7:1-8:22 have in common with 1:1-6:13? Consider especially 1:2-4, 2:6-9, 5:21, 6:9-13.

For Further Study: Add 7:1-8:22 to your outline now, or wait to do all of 7:1-12:6 at once.

12. What steps could you take to begin living more in light of this insight?

_____

_____

_____

_____

_____

_____

13. List any questions you have about 7:1-8:22.

_____

_____

_____

_____

For the group

Warm-up. Ask group members to think of some situation when they have been faced with a threat to home, job, or other security. How did they feel? How did they deal with the danger? Let one or two people respond briefly.

Read aloud.

Summarize. Ask someone to tell in a few sentences what happens in chapters 7-8 and what the point or message of the chapters is.

Immanuel. Looking for the reason why Ahaz disobeys God (question 2) is not mere speculation. God judges the motives behind outward acts, and while we may never be in Ahaz' situation, we may be able to identify with his wrong attitudes. Suggesting a biblical character's possible motives is proper as long as we are careful not to think that our theories are as authoritive as the passage's plain statements.

Avoid an argument over whether 7:14 had a first fulfillment in Isaiah's time. We include that interpretation as a plausible and widely held one, but still the sign's crucial meaning for us concerns Jesus' identity. Evangelical scholars on both sides of the double fulfillment debate agree that 7:14 points to Mary as a *virgin* when Jesus was born; the debate is whether an earlier virgin married, bore a child in the normal manner, and named him Immanuel.

You might want to summarize 7:1-25 and discuss applications before going on to chapter 8.

Fear God. One of the difficulties of studying prophecies is that they often assume that the hearers know all about the situation being addressed; it is like listening to one side of a stranger's telephone conversation. We don't know what "conspiracy" God meant in 8:12, but Isaiah did. Fortunately, we can guess well enough to see applications for ourselves.

Paint a brief picture of the circumstances Isaiah was facing: Aram and Israel were allied and threatening to invade unless Judah joined in their treaty; Jerusalem was full of political factions, most of whom would gladly have disposed of Isaiah; a treaty with Assyria promised disaster for Judah. The word "conspiracy" in 8:12 could equally mean "alliance," "treaty," or "faction." Try to identify with the emotions Isaiah may have felt in this situation.

Then look at the response God urges (questions 5-10). As chapter 7 focused on Ahaz' response to events, so chapter 8 focuses on Isaiah's. In both chapters, the name "the LORD is salvation" expresses the theme.

A key concept in chapter 8 is "the fear of the LORD." For many people, this conjures up the idea of cringing before a tyrant. If "God is love" and "perfect love drives out fear" (1 John 4:8,18), then it seems to some people that we should trust God, not fear Him. Help the group see the necessity of a healthy fear of the Sovereign Lord. How can you cultivate this attitude in your group?

Summarize. As usual, summarize both what you've learned and how it applies to you. If you have time, it would be helpful to trace common themes from chapters 1-6 to chapters 7-8, since Isaiah's message is a unity.

Wrap-up. Remind the group that 9:1-12:6 continues the section begun in 7:1. You could plan to discuss this week's applications at the beginning of your next meeting.

Worship. Thank God for the sign and gift of the Child. Thank Him for being the Rock. Tell Him your current fears, and ask Him to teach you how to fear Him.

Old Testament Prophets, part two

After the Exodus from Egypt, the Lord made a treaty, or *covenant*, with Israel like a treaty between an overlord and a subject people. The people agreed to serve and obey the Lord as God, and to accept the consequences of obedience and disobedience. The agreed consequences of obedience were blessings (Deuteronomy 4:32-40, 28:1-14), and the agreed consequences of disobedience were punishments (Deuteronomy 28:15-68).

Because the Lord was patiently training His people as a father trains his children (Hebrews 12:5-11), He did not simply let the consequences fall on each generation. Instead, He sent prophets in each generation to tell how well He thought the people were living up to the covenant and how He planned to respond. When the nation was disobedient, the Lord sent prophets like Isaiah to warn the people that the agreed results were going to occur unless they repented.

In this way, the people could never accuse the Lord of injustice. They had agreed to the standards of conduct and to the consequences, and the Lord never acted without ample forewarning and second chances.[7]

(continued on page 90)

---

1. Edward Young, *The Book of Isaiah*, volume 1 (Grand Rapids, Michigan: William B. Eerdmans Publishing Company, 1965), pages 286-289; *The NIV Study Bible*, page 1027; Leupold, volume 1, pages 155-157; Kidner, page 196.
2. Young, volume 1, pages 284-292; Matthew Henry.
3. Leupold, volume 1, pages 155-158; Kidner, page 596; *The NIV Study Bible*, page 1027.
4. Second Chronicles 32:30; *The NIV Study Bible*, page 1028.
5. *The NIV Study Bible*, page 1029.
6. Young, volume 1, pages 314-318; Kidner, page 597; Leupold, volume 1, pages 175-176.
7. Fee and Stuart, page 150.

ISAIAH 9:1-10:34

The Son of David

Chapter 8 ended in the blackness of war, anarchy, and spiritual confusion that consumed Israel and Judah in the eighth century BC. But the Lord gave Isaiah visions of what lay beyond the darkness—the end of Assyria, the survival of a faithful remnant, and a King who would restore peace, justice, and the knowledge of God. As you read 9:1-10:34, keep 7:1-8:22 and the outline on page 18 in mind.

A child is born (9:1-7)

The Assyrian army overran *Zebulun* and *Naphtali* (tribal territories in northern Israel) within months of Isaiah's meeting with Ahaz (7:1-9).[1] But just as these were the first lands of Israel to fall, so they would be the first to see the "great light." Zebulun and Naphtali were part of the region called *Galilee*, which became predominantly Gentile after Assyria deported the Israelites and replaced them with pagans. *The way of the sea, along the Jordan* was the ancient trade route through Galilee from Damascus to Egypt. (See the map on page 70.)

1. Read Isaiah 9:1-7 and Matthew 4:12-17. According to Matthew, how did Jesus begin to fulfill Isaiah's prophecy?

_____

_____

Map of Isaiah 9:1

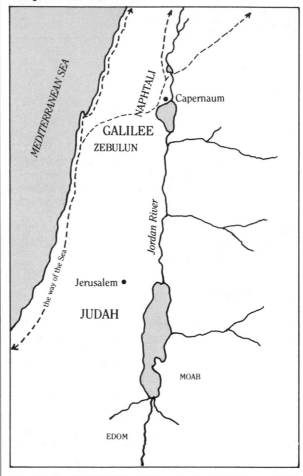

Midian's defeat (9:4). Gideon defeated invaders from Midian and broke their control over Israel (Judges 7:22-25).

Yoke . . . bar (9:4). Slavery to Assyria—or to anyone or anything—is like wearing the yoke of an ox (Isaiah 10:26-27).

Son (9:6). The Jews understood this to mean a descendant of the royal line of David. Luke 1:26-35 and 3:23-38 tell us more about this Son.

For Thought and Discussion: a. Why will warriors' clothes be burned when the Messiah reigns (9:5,7)?

b. What else do you learn about the Kingdom of God from 9:3-7?

2. When Jesus came, the Jews expected the Messiah (the promised King) to liberate their nation from the Romans and re-establish the earthly kingdom of Israel. What parts of 9:3-7 would have led the Jews to expect a Savior like this?

_____

_____

_____

_____

_____

_____

_____

For Further Study: Jesus will consummate Isaiah 9:1-7 when He returns to reign in glory. What do Luke 21:25-28 and Revelation 19:11-20:6 tell you about that final fulfillment?

3. Jesus did not meet the Jews' expectations. However, how did He begin to . . .

enlarge the nation (Isaiah 9:3; see also Ephesians 2:11-22)?

_____

_____

_____

_____

_____

shatter the yoke that burdens His people and break the rod of the oppressor (Isaiah 9:4; see also Luke 7:18-23, 8:43-48; Romans 6:6-7; Hebrews 2:14-15)?

_____

_____

_____

For Thought and Discussion: An ordinary king may be a counselor, a mighty man, a father to his people, and a prince (9:6). What makes this son unique?

Optional Application: How is Jesus' identity and mission as Wonderful Counselor, etc. relevant to your life?

_____

_____

_____

reign on David's throne with justice forever (Isaiah 9:7; see also Luke 11:20; 18:35-43; Colossians 1:13-14,18; 2:9-10)?

_____

_____

_____

_____

_____

Counselor (9:6). This Hebrew word can mean an advisor, but it can also mean one who plans, purposes, and carries out a plan of action[2] with wisdom.[3]

Peace (9:6,7). The Hebrew word *shalom* means wholeness and well-being in all aspects of life—health, harmony between people, prosperity, contentment, etc. It is not just the absence of war.

Justice, righteousness (9:7). See page 83.

4. Choose one of the things Isaiah says about the Son in 9:6-7, and explain why it seems especially important to you.

_____

_____

_____

_____

_____

_____

72

The Lord against Israel (9:8-10:4)

"Yet for all this, his anger is not turned away, his hand is still upraised."
                        Isaiah 9:12,17,21; 10:4

After a glimpse of the golden future in 9:1-7, we are now back between 732 and 722 BC. Assyria subdued Aram in 732 and turned Aram against Israel (9:12). The Philistines, too, are taking advantage of Israel's weakness after the Assyrian onslaught that has left only Samaria unravaged.

Surely the brush with destruction has taught Israel's leaders in Samaria a lesson. Surely the sudden loss of their mighty kingdom has moved them to humble themselves before the Lord. No, the Lord sees the attitudes in the Samaritans' hearts. In 9:8-10:4, Isaiah speaks God's indictment and proclaims His sentence. The fulfillment will come in 722 when Sargon smashes Samaria and deports its leaders.

Bricks . . . stone (9:10). Bricks made of sun-dried clay crumbled easily, but the stone with which rich people built was expected to last forever.

Fig trees . . . cedars (9:10). The sycamore fig was a scruffy tree with small value, but cedar took years to grow and was prized for its wood. It was common for armies to demolish houses and even cut down all the trees in a country to make the people destitute.

The conflagration of 9:18-21 came to pass. Invasions made farming impossible, so famine drove the depraved Israelites to eat extreme things. Leadership in Samaria degenerated into factional intrigue and assassination. Israel's two dominant tribes, Ephraim and Manasseh, fought over food and power. Eventually, near anarchy reigned until Assyria stopped it by depopulating the country.

Unjust laws . . . oppressive decrees (10:1). "Evil statutes" and "unjust decisions" in NASB. These

For Thought and Discussion: Why does God speak in 9:8-10:34 against Israel and Assyria? How do these judgments fit into the message of chapters 7-12?

For Further Study:
a. How were Israel's leaders thinking and planning in response to the country's almost total destruction (9:9-11)?
b. Why were the leaders' attitudes so offensive to God (9:9-11,13)?

For Further Study:
a. Neither Assyrian cruelty nor persistent raids by Aram and Philistia brought Israel to repentance (9:9-13). Whom did the Lord blame for the people's failure to repent (9:13-17)?
b. What was the Lord going to do about this situation (9:14-17)?

73

For Further Study:
Think about the two
causes of the "fire"
that consumed Israel
(9:18-19). What do
these tell you about
human choice and
God's sovereignty in
history's events of
judgment?

**For Thought and
Discussion:** a. Name
the four sins the Lord
judges in 9:9-10,
13-17, 18-21; and
10:1-2.
   b. Do these
verses contain any
warnings for nations
or individuals today?
If so, what are they?

**For Thought and
Discussion:** Why
was it absurd for
people to manipulate
the law to get rich
(10:1-4)? What was
scheming going to
get them?

**Optional
Application:** Does
9:8-10:4 convict you
in any areas (consider
9:10,13; 10:1)? If so,
how?

are rulings by judges, lawyers, and government
officials in legal cases.[4]

5. What do you learn about the Lord from
   9:8-10:4?

   what He expects of His people _____

   _____

   _____

   _____

   _____

   _____

   His character _____

   _____

   _____

   _____

   _____

   _____

The Lord against Assyria (10:5-34)

The Lord has been using Assyria to punish Israel
and Judah, but now He begins to show what lies
beyond this use: judgment for Assyria (10:5-19); the
deliverance of a faithful remnant (10:20-23); the
aggressor halted at the very edge of Jerusalem
(10:24-34).

*Calno . . . Carchemish . . . Hamath . . . Arpad
   . . . Samaria . . . Damascus* (10:9). Cities in
   Aram and Israel that submitted to Assyria
   between 732 and 717 BC.

Wasting disease (10:16). Verses 16-19 were partly
   fulfilled in 701 BC. King Sennacherib of Assyria
   sent his army to destroy Jerusalem, but a
   disease—probably a burning fever—decimated

74

the army as it approached Jerusalem (Isaiah 37:36). Then, political trouble forced Sennacherib to withdraw his army from Judah. It never returned.

Forests (10:18-19). Tall trees are a favorite metaphor for loftiness in Isaiah (2:13; 10:33-34). Assyria finally crumpled before Babylon between 612 and 605 BC.

Remnant (10:20-23). This theme was so important to Isaiah that he named his eldest son *Shear-Jashub*, "a remnant shall return" (7:3, 10:21). Isaiah's mission was to prophesy judgment until Judah was desolate, yet to affirm that a "holy seed" would survive (6:11-13). He had already beheld Judah ravaged by war and kept from oblivion only by God's mercy (1:9). And there was worse to come.

The promise of a remnant was based on the covenant. The Lord had made an everlasting treaty with Abraham to bless his descendants in the land of Canaan (Genesis 12:2-3, 17:1-10; Deuteronomy 7:7-10; Psalm 105:8-11). The Lord swore to be Israel's God, and Israel would be His treasured chosen people. As a faithful and just God, He would never break His covenant. Yet, as a righteous and holy God, He could not be intimate with corrupt people (Leviticus 19:2, Psalm 24:3-4, Habakkuk 1:13). Therefore, only faithful members of the covenant nation were truly God's people. The mass of Israel repeatedly rebelled and was punished, but God consistently spared a remnant to inherit the covenant—seventy in Joseph's day (Genesis 45:7), seven thousand in Elijah's (1 Kings 19:13-18).[5]

God kept the promise in Isaiah 10:20-23. Many people in Judah and Jerusalem died when Sennacherib invaded in 701 BC, but the city and a remnant of the people were saved (Isaiah 37:30-32). In 538, 458, and 432 BC, about fifty thousand Jews returned to Judah from exile in Babylon; Ezra 9:8 and Nehemiah 1:2 call these a remnant. The Apostle Paul observed God saving a remnant of the Jews in his own day. Most Jews were rejecting the proclamation that Jesus was the Christ, but a few were believing (Romans 9-11). Paul knew that the Lord would

For Thought and Discussion: a. Did Assyria's king know that he was the Lord's tool for disciplining His chosen people? What was the king's view of his conquests and himself (10:5-14)?

b. How does the king resemble modern rulers? Do you see any of his attitudes in yourself?

c. What do you learn about the Lord from His use of Assyria and from His words in 10:12,15-19?

d. How should Christians think and act in light of 10:12,15-19?

For Further Study: Study Paul's whole reasoning about the remnant saved by grace in Romans 9-11.

For Further Study: Do a word study on *remnant*. For instance, study these passages in context: 2 Chronicles 30:6; Isaiah 11:11-16, 14:22, 16:14, 17:3, 37:4; Jeremiah 23:3, 31:7, 40:11, 42:1-22; Micah 2:12, 5:7-9.

For Thought and Discussion: The Jews of Isaiah's day believed that God would protect them just because they were descendants of Abraham and David (compare Luke 3:7-8). How does Isaiah 10:20-23 disprove that belief?

For Further Study: Does the remnant principle apply to the Church? See Matthew 13:24-30.

Optional Application: Pray about the remnant. Ask God to enable you to be one of those who truly rely on the Holy One. Ask Him to be merciful to a remnant of Israel in your day. Praise Him for being faithful to His promises and to His own righteous character.

continue to call a remnant of Israel into the family of Christ because of His promise to Abraham (Romans 11:1-6,28-29).

6. What do you learn about God from the fact that . . .

He decimates Israel when the nation sins?

_____

_____

_____

_____

_____

He never utterly abandons Israel, but always saves a remnant?

_____

_____

_____

_____

_____

7. King Ahaz relied on Assyria to protect Judah. That alliance proved foolish—Assyria struck and plundered. How does the remnant act differently from Ahaz (10:20)?

_____

_____

_____

_____

8. How is Isaiah 10:20-23 relevant to our lives? (Consider your answers to questions 6 and 7.)

_____

_____

76

_____

_____

_____

_____

_____

Optional Application: The Lord urged His people to have faith and courage as an army marched on Jerusalem (10:24-34). Do your circumstances call for any similar response? Explain.

Midian . . . burden . . . yoke (10:26-27). The Lord enabled a small force of Israelites to defeat the Midianites (Judges 7:1-25).

Oreb (10:26). One of Midian's leaders. (See Judges 7:25, Isaiah 9:4.)

Rod . . . Egypt (10:26). "When Moses stretched out his hand over the Red Sea, the waters engulfed the chariots of Pharaoh"[6] (Exodus 14:26-28).

Aiath . . . Migron . . . (10:28-32). Isaiah describes the advance of an army over the last ten miles to Jerusalem. The Assyrian army actually marched from the southwest (36:2), but God gave the vision this way because Assyria was the dreaded power of the north. "The aim of the oracle is not, presumably, to inform [of the exact route Assyria was going to take] but to inspire [the people to be spiritually prepared]."[7]

Your response

9. How would you summarize what God is trying to tell His people in 7:1-10:34? (Consider 7:9,14; 8:9,12-13,17; 9:1-7; 10:24-25.)

_____

_____

_____

_____

_____

77

For Further Study:
Add 9:1-10:34 to your
outline, or wait until
you have finished
11:1-12:6.

**Optional
Application:** Some
good passages for
meditation are
9:6,10,13,16;
10:3,12-13,15,
20-23,24.

10. What one truth from 9:1-10:34 seems most relevant to your life?

_____

_____

_____

_____

_____

11. How does this truth apply to you? How do you
want it to affect your character, thoughts, and
actions?

_____

_____

_____

_____

_____

12. What can you do this week to take this insight
to heart and put it into practice?

_____

_____

_____

_____

_____

13. Write down any questions you have about
9:1-10:34.

_____

_____

_____

_____

For the group

This lesson skips lightly over God's judgment on
Israel and Assyria. Repeated prophesies of judgment
overwhelm many Christians, and also we have tried
to limit the length of this study. If you want to be
more thorough, you can take two meetings to cover
lesson six and have group members answer the
optional questions in a notebook.

Warm-up. Ask what "darkness" symbolizes to the
group. This will lead into 9:1-7.

Read aloud. You may not want to read all of
9:1-10:34, since the lesson focuses on 9:1-7 and
10:20-23.

Summarize. Ask someone to summarize 9:1-7,
9:8-10:4, and 10:5-34. Then have someone explain
as best he can how these passages relate to each
other and to chapters 1-8. Plan to return to these
questions after discussing 9:1-10:34.

A child is born. Questions 1-3 focus on how Jesus
fulfilled 9:1-7 in His first coming and is fulfilling it
now. If you like, you can discuss how He will consummate that prophecy at His second coming. We
have de-emphasized that because there is more
debate about events that haven't happened yet.
However, the future fulfillment may be important to
your group. Confidence about the future gives
encouragement in the present.

Give everyone a chance to share at least one
personal insight from 9:6-7 (question 4). You could
also discuss what "Wonderful Counselor," "Mighty
God," "Everlasting Father," and "Prince of Peace"
mean. Be sure to consider how Jesus' identity and
mission are relevant to your lives.

The Lord against Israel. Although much of 9:8-
10:34 is optional, these passages are part of Scripture and important to Isaiah's overall message. Feel
free to cover them more carefully. These passages
portray aspects of the Lord's character, and actions
and attitudes that anger Him—all of which are still
relevant today.

The Lord against Assyria. Here we have focused on
10:20-23 because it is important to both Isaiah's and

Paul's teaching. Be sure to grasp what the promise of the remnant in Isaiah is, and what it shows about God's character and plan. Look at Paul's use of the idea if you have time.

For more information about the remnant, see commentaries on Isaiah or Romans, or ask your pastor to recommend some books. Interpretations of Romans 9-11 vary.

Summarize.

Wrap-up. The next lesson makes use of the Christian practice of meditating on a phrase of Scripture, thinking about what it means and how it applies personally, and praying about it. Remind the group of the paragraph "Memorizing and Meditating" on page 7. Answer any questions the group has. Lesson seven should make itself clear, but if you read through it ahead of time, you can warn the group of any potentially confusing parts.

Worship. Praise God and Christ for what 9:1-10:34 reveals about each of Them. Thank Them for the government of peace, the judgment of sin, the remnant. Ask Christ to act in your life as Wonderful Counselor, Everlasting Father, etc.

1. *The NIV Study Bible*, page 1029; Kidner, page 597.
2. *The NIV Study Bible*, page 1030.
3. Young, volume 1, page 335.
4. Young, volume 1, page 355; Leupold, volume 1, page 198.
5. Technically, the seventy in Joseph's day were not a remnant of a larger group, but the number of Israelites God started with. However, Genesis uses the word *remnant* in 45:7. The people who survived the plagues in the wilderness, the battles in the time of the judges, the invasions under the kings, and the exiles are more properly called remnants, although Scripture does not always use the word.
6. *The NIV Study Bible,* page 1032.
7. Kidner, page 598.

LESSON SEVEN

ISAIAH 11:1-12:6

Salvation

While the Assyrian army was devastating Israel and terrorizing Judah, Isaiah spoke the prophecies of 11:1-12:6. As you read these chapters, imagine yourself hearing them while savage troops are marching toward your border.

The Branch (11:1-16)

Stump of Jesse (11:1). The Lord promised to lay Judah waste until the holy seed—the faithful remnant—was just a stump in the barren earth (6:13). Uzziah, Jotham, Ahaz, and Hezekiah belonged to the royal dynasty of David, the son of Jesse (1 Samuel 16:10-13). The family survived the Assyrian invasion of 701 BC by a miracle (Isaiah 37). It endured the Babylonian exile by another series of marvels. However, after the exile began in 586 BC, there was no Davidic king because Judah was never again an independent state. The line of David lay like a dormant seed, a lifeless stump. But Isaiah promised that the stump would someday sprout a king for Judah.

1. The Son of David differs from Judah's kings firstly in that "the Spirit of the LORD" rests on Him (11:2). The Spirit equips Him for His mission. What is the Son's mission (11:3-4)?

For Thought and Discussion: The lofty forest of Assyria will be leveled (10:18-19, 33-34), but the stump of Jesse will sprout (11:1). What is the Lord saying? Compare 2:11.

81

For Further Study:
Compare 7:14, 9:1-7, and 11:1-16. Observe how the promised Son is revealed from many angles.

For Thought and Discussion: Why does Christ not judge by what He sees and hears (11:3, 42:18-19)? How can someone make right decisions by ignoring what he sees and hears? (See Leviticus 19:15, John 7:24, James 2:1-10.)

For Thought and Discussion: Why does Jesus *delight* in the fear of God (11:3)? What are the implications here for us?

_____

_____

_____

_____

Counsel (11:2). Related to wisdom and understanding, but the accent in "counsel" is on the ability to plan and strategize, especially in warfare (see 9:6).[1] *Power* is the ability to carry out those plans.

Knowledge (11:2). In this context, intimacy with God and knowledge of spiritual truths.[2]

Fear of the Lord (11:2,3). A respect and awe of God that grows from intimate knowledge of His justice, holiness, goodness, and worthiness of honor. (See Proverbs 1:7, 9:10; Isaiah 8:13.)[3] Beholding the Lord ought to terrify even His faithful servants (Isaiah 6:1-5, Revelation 1:12-18).

2. Why does Christ need the Spirit's three-fold gift (11:2-3) in order to fulfill His mission (11:3-4)?

wisdom and understanding _____

_____

_____

_____

_____

counsel and power _____

_____

_____

_____

_____

knowledge and the fear of the Lord _____

_____

_____

_____

_____

_____

_____

For Thought and Discussion: To what extent has Christ already brought into being what 11:1-16 says about Him and His Kingdom? To what extent are these promises yet to be fulfilled?

Optional Application: Ask the Lord to give you the Spirit's gifts named in 11:2-3. Ask Him to teach you where you fall short in these areas and how you need these gifts to serve Him. Ask Him to teach you deeply what wisdom, counsel, etc. are.

Righteousness (11:4-5). The quality of being right is an essential character of God. His nature is the standard of right character and morality, and His will is the standard of right events and decisions. He displays His righteousness in the world by giving His righteous Law; being faithful to His covenants, promises, and plans; setting right what is wrong in the world by saving the righteous and punishing the wicked; and making sinners right again by providing sacrifices that atone for sin. The ultimate act of God's righteousness is offering His Son as the true atonement sacrifice and the true righteous ruler.

A human is righteous when he conforms to God's standards of what is right. This includes what is right for all people as well as what is fitting for that person's particular role. For instance, a righteous king implements justice according to God's laws.

God's righteous standard includes humility before God, dependence upon His power to deliver people from affliction, and dependence upon His atoning sacrifice to maintain His people's right relationship to Him. Isaiah 6:5-6 shows that this dependence was important even in Isaiah's time, when Christ's work was only foreshadowed.[4]

Optional Application: a. Ask God to teach you to delight in the fear of the Lord. Meditate on reasons to fear Him with delight. Psalms 34 and 130, Isaiah 6, and Revelation 1 may help your meditations.

b. How should the fear of the Lord affect your actions?

3. We are the Body of Christ. Jesus has given us His mission and the Spirit to equip us (John 20:21-23). How is Isaiah 11:1-5 relevant to us? How should it move us to think, pray, and act?

For Thought and Discussion: Why does peace naturally flourish when people know the Lord intimately (11:9)?

Optional Application: In the Lord's Prayer we pray, "your kingdom come" (Matthew 6:10). Expand on this request from the promises in Isaiah 11:1-12:6.

For Thought and Discussion: What does it mean for the earth to be full of the knowledge of the Lord (11:9)?

For Further Study: Compare Isaiah 11:6-9 to Romans 8:18-25. How should this future hope affect our attitudes and actions today?

4. What will result when Christ governs justly, punishes the wicked, and models right attitudes toward God (11:6-9)?

5. What else will happen when Christ reigns (11:10-16)?

6. In its fullest extent, 11:3-16 has not yet taken place. Still, why is it important for us to know these things? What difference should they make to our lives?

**Study Skill—Prophetic Forms:
The Promise Oracle**

Isaiah 2:1-5, 4:2-6, 9:1-7, and 11:1-16 follow a form called the *promise* or *salvation* oracle. The form includes reference to the future ("In that day . . . ," (2:2, 4:2, 11:10), radical change (the nations seeking God, the end of war), and blessing. The blessings are the ones promised in the covenant (Deuteronomy 28:1-14)—life, health, prosperity, agricultural abundance, respect, and safety.[5] Salvation oracles and woe oracles occur side by side in Isaiah.

These passages do not answer all of our questions about heaven, the millenium, and so on. Therefore, we need to study them for what they do tell us, and look for answers to our other questions in other passages. When the Lord chooses not to satisfy our curiosity, we need to be content to wait.

Also, in promise oracles the Lord frequently uses symbolism to make His point. For instance, beating swords into plowshares (2:4) vividly depicts the end of war, and the "Branch" (4:2) symbolizes either Christ or the holy people that grows from Him. On the other hand, the Lord also speaks literally in promise oracles. Therefore, when we try to unravel promise oracles, we should use the Lord's guidance, other passages of Scripture, and common sense to determine when the Lord is speaking literally and when symbolically, and what the symbols mean. Even if we cannot be certain about our understanding of the details, the overall point of the prophecy is clear enough to motivate us to act in faith today.

Songs of salvation (12:1-6)

When the wonders of 11:1-16 have come to pass, what will there be left to do but sing songs of praise? The people of Isaiah's time were at enmity with God, beset by fears, starving for spiritual and physical nourishment. But observe the changes "in that day."

7. Read through 12:1-6 meditatively, dwelling on phrases that strike you. What is true of a person God has saved (12:1-3)?

_____

_____

_____

_____

_____

_____

8. What does it mean that God is your "strength" and your "song" (12:2)?

_____

_____

_____

_____

_____

_____

Salvation (12:2-3). Negatively, this means deliverance from danger, sickness, loss, slavery, and all other evils. Positively, it means the restoration and preservation of safety, health, wholeness, and all other blessings.

9. What does it mean to "draw water from the wells of salvation" (12:3)? (*Optional:* See Psalm 36:9; Jeremiah 2:13; John 4:10,13-14.)

_____

_____

_____

_____

_____

10. What is the natural response to what God has done for us (12:4-6)?

_____

_____

_____

_____

Your response

11. Since chapter 13 begins a new section, this is a good time to review. How would you summarize God's message in 7:1-12:6? (You might review your summaries on pages 65 and 77.)

_____

_____

_____

_____

_____

_____

12. Summarize what you have learned about Christ from 7:14, 9:1-7, and 11:1-16.

_____

_____

_____

_____

_____

_____

Optional Application: Meditate on:

  a. how God is your strength, your song, your salvation.

  b. how He has ended His anger and comforted you.

  c. His wells of salvation.

For Thought and Discussion: How does Isaiah's name ("The LORD is salvation") relate to 11:1-12:6?

For Thought and Discussion: What impressions about God does Isaiah 1:1-12:6 give you?

13. What aspect of 11:1-12:6 would you like to concentrate on this week?

_____

_____

_____

_____

_____

14. How would you like this insight to affect your life? What implications does it have?

_____

_____

_____

_____

_____

15. What steps can you take to begin letting this insight affect you?

_____

_____

_____

_____

_____

16. List any questions you have about 11:1-12:6.

_____

_____

_____

_____

88

For the group

Warm-up. Ask group members what ideas or pictures come to mind when they think of salvation.

Read aloud.

Summarize.

The Branch. This lesson is a bit shorter and more meditative than previous ones, so you can catch your breath and practice approaching the Scriptures in different ways. You could cover 11:1-16 by looking at phrases in turn and discussing what they mean. Then step back and discuss what impressions of Christ and of God's Kingdom the whole of 11:1-12:6 gives you.

Remind the group that because you live after Jesus' first coming and before His second, 11:1-12:6 is partially fulfilled and true of the Kingdom you inhabit, but it is partly yet to be fulfilled when Jesus returns. Help the group to see the already-but-not-yet aspects of 11:1-12:6. What differences do these promises make to your present lives?

Songs of salvation. This section focuses on God's character and our response in a meditative, personal way. These songs lend themselves to quiet reflection on one phrase at a time. Urge group members to choose a phrase to meditate on during the coming week. You could allow time to share any fresh insights and applications on these phrases at the beginning of your next meeting.

If meditating on a phrase of Scripture is new to some people, refer to the description on page 7. Let group members voice any questions.

Summarize. Since chapter 13 begins a new section of the book, try to summarize Isaiah's message in chapters 1-12. What ideas and topics have recurred? How do the promises fit together with the woes?

Wrap-up. Isaiah 13:1-23:18 is a collection of woes against the pagan nations around Judah. If you would like to do a thorough study of those prophecies, plan a week or two to cover part or all of the Optional Lesson on pages 203-210. If you have had enough of judgment, or if your time is limited, have the group read page 91 and then move on to lesson eight. (Encourage everyone to read 13:1-23:18 if possible.)

Worship. Pray your own songs of praise along the lines of 12:1-6. Focus on the characters of God and Christ as revealed in 1:1-12:6.

Old Testament Prophets, part three

Isaiah's job was to call the nation back to faith. While this included convicting the people of rebelling against the covenant, it also included encouragement to hope in God. Both judgment and promise were essential.

One difficulty we have in understanding Isaiah is that when the Lord gave him visions of the future, He did not tell the prophet how far in the future various events would be. Isaiah wrote as though prophecies of the day of the Lord would all be fulfilled nearly simultaneously. From our perspective, however, we can see long stretches of time between the destruction of Assyria, the first coming of Christ, and His return. So, when we read Isaiah's prophecies we need to ask ourselves what has already occurred and what is still yet to occur.

---

1. *The NIV Study Bible,* page 1033; Kidner, page 598.
2. Young, volume 1, page 382; Kidner, page 598.
3. *The NIV Study Bible,* page 1033; Young, volume 1, pages 382-383.
4. Horst Seebass and Colin Brown, "Righteousness, Justification," *The New International Dictionary of New Testament Theology,* volume 3, edited by Colin Brown (Grand Rapids, Michigan: Zondervan Corporation, 1978), pages 354-358.
5. Fee and Stuart, page 160.

ISAIAH 13:1-23:18

Oracles Against the Nations

In an era when people believed that each nation had its own gods who could not meddle in other gods' countries, Isaiah proclaimed the Lord to be King over all nations. Moreover, said Isaiah, He is King not just in the abstract but in the specific events of each nation and life. This is the message of 13:1-23:18, a collection of oracles against pagan nations that Isaiah uttered at various times during his ministry.

These chapters can overwhelm us with references to events we don't know and with constant tones of wrath. So, since this may be your first time through the book of Isaiah, we've made a thorough study of 13:1-23:18 optional. In the Optional Lesson on pages 203-210, you will find background on each of the oracles in these chapters to help you understand what Isaiah is talking about. You will also find some questions on each oracle. We hope you will want to work carefully through all the oracles at some time, for each one has valuable lessons about God's character and what He desires of His people. You might enjoy studying at least one or two of the oracles along with lesson eight.

Oracle (13:1). A "divine declaration."[1] KJV reads "burden." A biblical oracle is often, but not necessarily, a judgment.

---

1. Young, volume 1, pages 408-409.

ISAIAH 24:1-27:13, 33:1-12, 34:1-17

The King of the World

Isaiah 13:1-23:18 makes it clear that the Lord is sovereign over every event in every nation. Pride, cruelty, or self-centeredness in any nation is an offense against His justice. The judgments prophesied for individual nations now lead in chapter 24 to a promise of holocaust for the whole world. But 24:1-27:13 looks beyond the judgment to glory.

In these chapters, Isaiah interweaves prophecies of judgment, the blessings of the Kingdom beyond judgment, and praise to God for those blessings. For brevity's sake, we will look at each topic in turn. Lesson eight will cover the judgments, and lesson nine will explore the blessings of the Kingdom and the songs of praise. However, you may find it easier to sort out the Lord's message if you read 24:1-27:13 before beginning on the questions below. Also, glance at the outline on page 19 to see how 13:1-23:18 and 24:1-27:13 fit into Isaiah's book.

The whole earth devastated
(24:1-23, 25:10-12, 26:20-21, 34:1-17)

Everlasting covenant (24:5). After the great Flood, the Lord made a covenant with Noah similar to a typical Near Eastern royal grant. The Lord promised never to destroy all earthly life with a flood (Genesis 9:8-17). This was an unearned grant, and Noah's descendants inherited it

93

For Further Study:
Why is there a con-
nection between
human sin and the
earth's curse? See
Genesis 1:28, 2:15,
3:17-18; Romans
8:18-21.

**For Thought and
Discussion: a.** Will
social distinctions
make any difference
in the time of crisis
(24:2)?

b. What implica-
tions should this fact
have for our lives?

**Optional
Application:** Pray for
the earth defiled by
humans (24:5). Pray
for people you know
who are in danger of
destruction. Ask God
to be swift and merci-
ful in judgment, and
praise Him as in
24:14-16.

automatically. However, they could reject the
covenant by persistently abusing their authority
over other living creatures and their duties to
the Lord. In 24:5, Isaiah implies that mankind
has done just that, so the Lord will rend the
earth.[1] Even though the Gentiles did not know
God's full Law, they had His law of basic right
and wrong, so they were obligated to keep God's
covenant with Noah.[2]

1. How does Isaiah describe the condition of the
   earth in the last days (24:1-6)?

   _____

   _____

   _____

   _____

   _____

   _____

2. What caused this condition (24:5-6)?

   _____

   _____

   _____

3. Does the state of the earth and its people in
   24:5-6 resemble the modern world in any ways?
   If so, give some examples.

   _____

   _____

   _____

   _____

   _____

   _____

   _____

4. The consequences of persistent rebellion against God's lordship are graphically described in 24:1-4,6-13,16-20. What else will happen on the day of destruction (24:21-23)?

_____

_____

_____

The vineyard again (27:2-11)

As you read this song, recall 5:1-7.

5. How does the Lord treat Israel, His vineyard (27:3)?

_____

_____

_____

_____

6. If His vines were just briers and thorns, the Lord wouldn't mind simply burning them up and starting again (27:4). But He hates to do that to good grape vines even though they are barren. What does He wish His vines—His people—would do (27:5)?

_____

_____

_____

_____

7. Why won't the Lord burn up His vines (27:6)?

_____

_____

_____

_____

For Thought and Discussion: Why is 24:14-16 a reasonable response to 24:6-13?

For Further Study: Isaiah 34:1-17 is a judgment on Edom, a nation bordering Judah. Edom often symbolizes the whole pagan world. What does God say to Edom? Why is He so harsh?

For Further Study:
Luke 13:6-9, John
15:1-8, and Revela-
tion 3:14-16 may
shed some light on
Isaiah 27:2-6.

8. What message does 27:2-6 offer Christians?

_____

_____

_____

_____

_____

_____

Atoned for (27:9). "Forgiven" in NASB. To atone is
to make satisfaction, to cover a debt. A price
must be paid. Israel offered blood sacrifices to
atone for sin, but sometimes additional action
was necessary.

Altar stones . . . Asherah poles . . . incense altars
(27:9). The Canaanite god Baal was often worshiped at stone altars built on hills, called "high
places." A wooden pillar commonly stood
nearby to symbolize the presence of the goddess
Asherah, Baal's consort. Incense, as well as
animal sacrifice, was a normal offering. Israel
participated in idolatrous worship continually,
despite the prophets' warnings.

---

9. What price must Israel (Jacob) pay in order to
atone for the people's sin (27:9)?

_____

_____

_____

_____

10. What inner commitment do these actions
represent? (*Optional:* See Exodus 20:1-6.)

_____

_____

96

11. Jesus has forever replaced the blood sacrifices for atonement (Hebrews 10:1-14). Yet, do we need to do what Isaiah 27:9 describes? Why or why not?

_____

_____

_____

_____

_____

_____

Optional Application: Do you need to make peace with God (27:5) or smash some of your idols (27:9)? If so, ask God to enable you to do this. Ask Him to cleanse your sin and help you to keep resisting the temptation of idolatry (Ephesians 3:14-21, 4:22-24; 1 John 1:8-2:2).

Prayer (33:1-12)

Isaiah pronounces woe upon the destroyer (33:1) and mourns the waste the traitor has caused (33:7-12). The righteous are caught in the destroyer's ruin and await God's vengeance.

12. How do the righteous respond while they await God's judgment (33:2-6)?

_____

_____

_____

_____

13. Why do they respond like this?

_____

_____

_____

97

_____

_____

_____

Your response

14. What insight from 24:1-27:11 or 33:1-12 currently seems most significant to you?

_____

_____

_____

_____

_____

15. How would you like this truth to affect you?

_____

_____

_____

_____

16. What steps can you take this week toward applying this insight to your life?

_____

_____

_____

_____

_____

_____

17. List any questions you have about anything in
this lesson.

_____

_____

_____

_____

For the group

Warm-up. Ask, "Is there anything in your life that
you are tempted to make more important than the
Lord?" This will lead to 27:9.

Read aloud.

Summarize. What is the main message that runs
through all of the prophecies in this lesson?

Questions. This lesson swiftly covers some important concepts—human sin and the earth's curse
(questions 1-3), the judgment upon fallen angels
(question 4), lukewarmness (questions 5-8), and
atonement (questions 9-11). You could easily devote
a whole meeting just to one or two of these, especially if you discuss some of the optional questions.

The cross-references in the "For Further Study"
on page 94 should help explain the connection
between human sin and the earth's curse. This may
be a new notion for many people. How does it affect
your view of ecology?

The judgment of the angels (24:21-23) fasci-
nates many people, but God mentions it only in
passing in Isaiah. Refer interested people to Ephesians 6:11-12 and Revelation 20:7-10.

Isaiah 27:2-6 is difficult. You might need a
commentary to make sense of it. Compare Revelation 3:14-16, where God complains that the church
is neither hot (making peace) nor cold (briers and
thorns).

For questions 9-11, recall the meaning of
atonement (27:9) from lesson four (6:7). It is startling that God says Israel can do something that will
pay the price for its sin. But notice that the price is
repentance and rejection of sin—a tall order. Also,

the need for a sacrifice for sin is assumed by Isaiah's Jewish audience. We need Jesus for both repentance and sacrifice.

Summarize.

Wrap-up.

Worship. The Lord presents a grim face in this section, but it should bring joy to all those who trust in Christ's atonement for sin and who sincerely live in hope of His reign. Praise God for His sovereignty over the nations and the spiritual powers, over world history and your personal lives. Praise Him for His hatred of sin and His gracious solution in Christ.

1. *The NIV Study Bible,* pages 19, 1049; Kidner, page 604.
2. Young, volume 2, page 157.

ISAIAH 24:1-27:13, 32:1-35:10

Restoration

Lesson eight was grim—the Lord plans to destroy the whole world for its wickedness. But by interweaving that promise with glimpses of the Kingdom that will follow the devastation, Isaiah shows that God's character as Judge is inseparable from His mercy. In this lesson, we will go back through 24:1-27:13 to see the restoration God plans. Then we will explore the same theme in 32:1-35:10, the exultant climax of part one of Isaiah's book.

Skim over 24:1-27:13 and 32:1-35:10 before you begin the questions. Also, refresh your memory with the outline on page 19.

For Further Study:
On the Kingdom, see Matthew 5:1-12, 13:24-52; Revelation 19:6-9, 21:1-8, 22:1-7; and Isaiah 27:12-13.

Predictions of the Kingdom

1. What will be the chief feature of the Kingdom of God (24:23)?

_____

_____

_____

2. According to 25:6-8, what else will be true in God's Kingdom?

_____

_____

_____

Optional Application: Meditate on 32:15-17. Ask God to pour out His Spirit on you to produce the righteous character that leads to peace. Make this a persistent prayer. What signs of unrighteousness do you see in your life? Ask God to uproot them.

3. One important prediction is repeated in 25:8 and 26:19. What is it?

4. Chapter 32 recalls the predictions of the Messiah in 9:1-7 and 11:1-16, but instead of describing the King, it describes His effect on His subjects.

   What will be true of the King's people when He reigns in righteousness (32:1-8)?

5. a. The women of Isaiah's day were "complacent" (32:9). They felt secure in the apparent peace that followed Sennacherib's retreat. But Isaiah promised that peace (wholeness, well-being, health, prosperity) was going to be impossible for a long time (32:9-14).

   What was going to have to change in the people's lives for true peace to be possible (32:15-17)?

102

b. Why is righteousness a prerequisite for peace and confidence (32:17)?

_____

_____

_____

_____

_____

For Further Study:
a. What happens to an unrighteous person who comes into the presence of the God who is a consuming fire (Malachi 4:1, Matthew 3:12)?

b. What happens to the person who wants to be righteous (Malachi 3:2-3, 4:2)?

6. Does 32:15-17 have implications for your life? If so, what are they?

_____

_____

_____

_____

_____

7. a. To live in God's Kingdom means to live in the King's presence. How does 33:14 describe the presence of God? (*Optional:* Compare Hebrews 12:29.)

_____

_____

_____

b. What sort of person can bear the presence of such a Holy God (Isaiah 33:15-16; recall 6:5-7)?

_____

_____

_____

_____

_____

**Optional
Application:** How
can you become more
like what 33:15-16
portrays? Ask God to
show you some spe-
cific ways. For motiva-
tion, meditate on
33:17-24.

8. Jesus said, "Blessed are the pure in heart, for
they will see God" (Matthew 5:8). What does
Isaiah 33:17-24 say that the pure in heart will
see?

_____

_____

_____

_____

_____

9. Do you fall short of 33:15 in any ways? If so,
how?

_____

_____

_____

_____

_____

Lebanon . . . Carmel . . . Sharon (35:2). These
were the most fertile parts of Palestine. Israel
was a land of stark contrasts; arid regions barely
grew scrub, while Sharon bore rich crops and
Lebanon was famed for its huge cedars. ***Water***
(35:6) was a precious and rare commodity for
shepherds who tried to make a living near the
wilderness.
   Jackals (35:7) roamed the wilderness, living on carcasses. ***Grass and reeds and papyrus***
grew only in lakes and marshes.

Highway (35:8). "In ancient times, certain roads
between temples were open only to those who
were ceremonially pure."[1] In 11:16 and again in
40:3, the highway is the path on which God's
holy ones proceed from the land of bondage to
the promised land.

Lion (35:9). An ancient highway was not a paved
four-lane freeway for cars. It was a dirt path for

caravans of camels, donkeys, and people on foot. Among the many dangers of travel through deserted areas were wild animals hunting prey. The lion was the fiercest of these.

Study Skill—Lions In Zion?

Isaiah 11:6-7 tells us that in the Kingdom of God, lions will eat straw and sleep peacefully with calves. Isaiah 35:9 says there won't be any lions near Zion's highway. Is Isaiah confused?

In the Western world, we might hear several responses. Some say, " These passages contradict each other. The Bible is fallible." Others say, "Isaiah doesn't mean *real* lions. These verses are just symbols of a spiritual reality. The *real* Kingdom is people living in peace." Others use logic to harmonize the statements: "Lions that eat straw are in one sense lions and in another sense not lions."

A Hebrew would think differently. To him, the word *lion* represents a physical creature with the characteristic nature of "lionness." In prophetic poetry, a lion is both a physical animal and a symbol—the fiercest, most deadly predator Israel knows. The Hebrew would assume Isaiah is talking about physical lions. But the important thing would be the essence of what the lions are: lionness. Both 11:6-7 and 35:9 assert that lionness will be absent.

Why doesn't Isaiah just say, "Nothing fierce or dangerous will be there"? Because he is painting word-pictures that speak to the heart, not defining data that explain to the mind. *Lion* evokes the physical, spiritual, and symbolic all at once. So, instead of trying to nail down data about the Kingdom, try exploring what each image means. The Kingdom of God is a banquet (25:6), a tranquil farm (32:18-20), a blossoming desert (35:1-2), a land of transformed lions (11:6-7) and no lions at all (35:9).

10. Chapter 35 introduces many of the images of restoration that recur in chapters 40-66. What

105

For Thought and Discussion: Why do you suppose Isaiah includes predictions of the judgment of unbelievers (25:10-12) in songs of praise? Why should God be praised for judging and punishing?

do the following descriptions tell you about God's Kingdom?

the desert transformed into blossom (35:1-2; 6-7)

_____

_____

_____

_____

_____

the blind, deaf, dumb, and lame healed (35:5-6)

_____

_____

_____

_____

_____

the highway and its singing pilgrims (35:8-10)

_____

_____

_____

_____

_____

Praises

11. Prayerfully read 24:14-16; 25:1-5,9; and 26:1-15. As you read, write down what you observe about the following:

    God—His nature and acts, the traits that make Him praiseworthy

    _____

    _____

106

_____

_____

_____

_____

_____

how God's people should act in light of His
deeds and character

_____

_____

_____

_____

_____

_____

_____

Your response

12. What currently seems to be the most significant
    insight you have gained from studying
    24:1-27:13 and 32:1-35:10?

_____

_____

_____

_____

_____

13. How is this truth relevant to your life? How
    would you like it to affect your attitudes and
    habits?

_____

_____

**For Thought and
Discussion:** What
does it mean in prac-
tice to trust the Lord?
Why are 25:9 and
26:3-10 appropriate
responses to God's
character?

**For Thought and
Discussion:** In
26:10, Isaiah says
that the wicked per-
son ignores God's
majesty and upholds
his own pride, despite
the "grace" (NASB:
"favor") God shows
him. How do even
wicked people expe-
rience God's grace?

**Optional
Application:** Take
some time to think
about 26:3-4 and
26:7-9. How could
you apply one aspect
of these verses to
your life this week?
Plan to meditate daily
on one or more of
these verses, and to
look for situations in
which to act on them.

**Optional
Application:** Read
1 Peter 1:13. How
can you actively set
your hope on what
Isaiah 24:1-27:13,
32:1-35:10 prom-
ises? How should this
future hope affect
your present choices
and attitudes?

_____

_____

_____

14. What steps can you take to begin putting this
    into practice?

_____

_____

_____

_____

_____

15. List any questions you have about 24:1-27:13 or
    32:1-35:10.

_____

_____

_____

_____

_____

For the group

Warm-up. Ask the group, "If you were going to fix
one thing about the world, what would you
change?"

Read aloud. You will probably want to choose only
portions of these chapters to read aloud. But do read
at least a little. This is very helpful for refreshing
memories.

Summarize. What message do all these passages
have in common?

Questions. In these chapters, God is painting pictures of what His Kingdom will be like. He speaks
in terms that will be familiar to Palestinian peasants
and rich for modern urban Christians. Opinions vary

as to which statements are poetic metaphors for spiritual truths, which are literal, and which have both literal and figurative meanings. Also, westerners find difficult the Hebrew concept that the name of a thing (for example, "lion") means more than just the physical object. Ask God to show you what He wants to say about His Kingdom through such pictures as the banquet and the blooming desert. In what ways are these partly fulfilled in our lives? In what ways are they yet to come? If necessary, refer the group back to the Study Skill on page 85 as well as to the one on page 105. If this question of literal and figurative confuses some people's convictions about the accuracy of Scripture, then drop it.

As you explore the Kingdom's characteristics, remember to discuss what differences they make to your present lives. Consider 1 Peter 1:13—how does your future hope affect your present lives? These insights may motivate new action or renewed commitment to applications you began in past weeks. Also, how do your current lives call for *trust* (25:9, 26:3)? How can you grow in trust? How can you help each other grow in trust? Or, how can you grow in *purity of heart*?

Summarize.

Wrap-up.

Worship. Use the phrase "your kingdom come" from the Lord's Prayer as a springboard for prayer about God's Kingdom. Use the praises from question 11 to prompt your own praises.

1. *The NIV Study Bible*, page 1065.

ISAIAH 28:1-31:9

God's Help or Man's?

In chapters 7-12 we read Isaiah's words to Judah under Ahaz. Isaiah spoke hopeful promises of the Messiah to turn an ungodly king from trusting in Assyria. In chapters 13-27 we saw prophecies against many nations, culminating in judgment on the whole earth and deliverance for those who trust only in the Lord. Now, in chapters 28-39 we find Isaiah speaking to Judah under a new king, Hezekiah.

Ahaz did appeal to Assyria for safety, so Israel has been destroyed and Judah staggers under heavy tribute payments. The economy is fragile. War looms. People are anxiously intent on survival. Hezekiah's counselors urge him to ally with Egypt to escape Assyria. Once again, only one voice dissents from this policy: the man named "the LORD is salvation." Isaiah is now the trusted friend and chaplain of a godly but unwise king. He pronounces a series of "woes" to urge Hezekiah not to take the pro-Egyptian faction's advice.

Yet these chapters transcend their immediate political context. Of the many themes we could explore, we will concentrate on just one: the choice of where a nation or person should seek security. Read the whole passage before you begin the questions, in order to follow the flow of the prophecies.

For Further Study: Look at the outline on page 19 to see how the chapters in this lesson fit together. Ask the Lord to speak to you about your own life through this section.

Study Skill—Prophetic Oracles
Prophetic books often seem disjointed; the train of thought seems to shift abruptly. This
(continued on page 112)

For Thought and Discussion: How is the Lord a different kind of wreath for the believing remnant than Samaria was? Compare 28:3-4 to 28:5-6.

Optional Application: How are the Lord's traits in 28:5-6 relevant to your current needs?

(continued from page 111)
happens because a book like Isaiah's was not written all at once like one of Paul's letters. Rather, Isaiah's book is a collection of oracles he spoke at different times. A given section like 28:1-31:9 probably includes prophecies given over a year's time or more.

The Hebrew text does not indicate where one oracle ends and another begins. A single prophecy might be as short as two verses or as long as a chapter. We have to rely on the Holy Spirit, common sense, and careful study to follow the train of thought.

Woe (28:1, 29:1, 29:15, 30:1, 31:1, 33:1). The six woes in these chapters seem to be repeated for an intentional emphasis. Chapter 28 is addressed at first to the northern kingdom of Israel, but it shifts to Judah's leaders in verses 7-29. Chapters 29-31 are spoken to Hezekiah's advisers in Jerusalem, and chapter 33 pronounces woe upon Assyria and all future persecutors of God's people.

Wreath (28:1,3). Samaria, Ephraim's capital, was a lovely city built on a hill. Isaiah likened it to a crown of flowers that a reveler might wear at a banquet.

Do and do . . . (28:10,13). Isaiah 28:7-8 describes Israel's religious leaders, drunk with wine rather than filled with God's Spirit (Ephesians 5:18). Isaiah 28:9-10 is their "mocking response"[1] to Isaiah's warnings, and 28:11-13 is his "ominous rejoinder."[2] J. B. Phillips translates 28:9-10, "Are we just weaned. . . . Do we have to learn that The-law-is-the-law-is-the-law, The-rule-is-the-rule-is-the-rule . . . ?"[3] The Hebrew sounds like sing-song—the babbling of a fool, a foreigner, or a nag.

1. Examine 28:5-6,12 and 30:15.

    a. What blessings does the Lord offer His people in these verses?

112

_____

_____

_____

_____

b. How can the people obtain these good
things?

_____

_____

_____

_____

_____

Rest (28:12, 30:15). God wove a pattern of work and
rest into His creation and ordained it as a cycle
His people should follow (Exodus 20:8-11).
Israel was supposed to rest every seven days and
let fields lie fallow every seven years (Leviticus
25:1-7). These Sabbath-rests in part symbolized
that the Lord had freed His people from slave
labor in Egypt and promised them rest in
Canaan (Deuteronomy 5:12-15, Joshua 1:13).
God called the land of Israel the people's "resting place" and "inheritance" (Deuteronomy
12:9-10). But Israel had rest from war and
struggle only briefly under Joshua and later
Solomon (Joshua 21:43-45, 1 Kings 5:4). Otherwise, the nation was in constant turmoil, as
God promised would happen if the people disre-
garded His commands. The Sabbath day and
year were ignored in the interest of profits; idolatry flourished; violent injustice was rampant
(1 Kings 21:1-29; Jeremiah 7:9, 17:19-27).
Therefore, as Psalm 95:7-11 predicted and
Hebrews 3:7-4:11 quoted, Israel never attained
the full Sabbath-rest that God had planned.
That rest—security, safety, peace of mind—is
now available to whomever will be faithful and
obedient to Jesus (Matthew 11:28-30; Hebrews
3:18-19, 4:9-11).

For Thought and Discussion: In view of the people's attitudes, how did God regard their religious practices, and why (29:1-3,13-14)?

2. Israel needed rest from war, injustice, economic instability, strife between people, and spiritual turmoil. What kinds of rest do you need?

_____

_____

_____

_____

_____

Covenant with death (28:15,18). Judah's leaders had been making alliances with Egypt and plans for war, but from God's point of view these were nothing else than treaties or covenants with death and falsehood. The leaders may have been making idolatrous covenants in black rites, but more probably Isaiah was pointing out the true nature of their political schemes.[4]

3. What wrong means of obtaining security and prosperity did Judah's leaders use?

28:14-15 _____

_____

_____

29:15-16 _____

_____

_____

30:12 _____

_____

30:1-2,16; 31:1 _____

_____

_____

114

4. How did people in Israel and Judah regard God's law, prophetic revelation, and instruction?

28:9-10 _____

_____

_____

29:13 _____

_____

_____

30:8-12 _____

_____

_____

31:1 _____

_____

_____

5. Do you ever do anything like what you described in questions 3 and 4? If so, explain.

_____

_____

_____

_____

_____

Optional Application: What practical steps can you take to avoid treating God's Word as the leaders of Israel and Judah did?

For Further Study: To clarify Isaiah 29:13, see how Jesus applies it to the Pharisees in Matthew 15:1-11.

For Thought and Discussion: What happened to Judah because the people trusted other sources of security besides the Lord (28:11-19; 29:9-14; 30:3-5, 12-17)? How is this a warning for us today?

Ariel (29:1,2,7). Most commentators think this is the Hebrew word for "altar hearth" (see 29:2 in NIV). Others suggest "Lion of God" (NASB margin). Jerusalem was the place of God's altar, where offerings of atonement, fellowship, and thanks were burnt. But 29:1-24 makes the symbol of intimacy a symbol of holocaust— Jerusalem will be consumed to atone for her sins; the substitute sacrifices she has abused will no longer be accepted.[5]

For Thought and Discussion: Why is it foolish to rely on anything or anyone other than the Lord?

For Thought and Discussion: a. Is it safe to stop relying on military strength without trusting utterly in the Lord (31:1-3)? Why or why not?
   b. Is this relevant to your own nation's decisions? How, or why not?

6. What happens when Israel . . .

rejects God's words (28:11,13; 29:9-10)?

_____

_____

_____

_____

makes a covenant with death and lies (28:14-19)?

_____

_____

_____

_____

trusts in human intellect (29:14)?

_____

_____

_____

_____

trusts in military arms and allies (30:16-17, 31:1-3)?

_____

_____

_____

_____

7. What can we learn from these results of Israel's choices?

_____

_____

_____

_____

_____

_____

_____

8. Why does the Lord get so angry when we try to rely on something other than Him? (*Optional:* See Exodus 20:1-6.)

_____

_____

_____

_____

_____

For Further Study:
a. Compare Isaiah 28:16-19 and 30:12-13 to Luke 6:46-49. How are Jesus' and Isaiah's warnings alike and different?

b. How could your building grow more able to withstand God's tests?

c. What further light does 1 Corinthians 3:10-17 shed?

Optional Application: How do 28:16-17 and 30:12-13 apply to the ways you build in God's Church and your personal life?

A stone (28:16). In 8:14 the Lord is the stone; in 28:16 He lays it. Ephesians 2:17-22 and 1 Peter 2:4-10 explain the paradox: Christ is the Lord (God the Son) and the Stone whom the Lord (God the Father) lays.[6]

Like a high wall (30:13). In 28:16-17, the Lord defines the proper foundation and measures by which He will judge between good and bad building of the nation. A secure nation is like a well-built wall, a wall built on a solid foundation according to a true measuring line and plumb line (28:16-17). But a nation built according to oppression and deceit (28:17-18, 30:12-13) is like a cracked and bulging wall, ready to collapse suddenly under the tests God will send (30:13).

In 28:14-19, God promises hail and flood will come upon Israel. Some people will have built upon the *cornerstone* for a *sure foundation* and will have built according to the *measuring line* and *plumb line*. Those people will survive the flood. The rest will be swept away.

Optional Application: Reread 28:5-6,12,16; 30:15; 31:1. Choose one or two of those verses to meditate on for the next week. How could you apply one of them to your life?

For Thought and Discussion:
a. Summarize the message of 28:1-31:9.

b. How does this passage relate to 24:1-27:13? To 32:1-35:10? To the themes of the book of Isaiah?

Your response

9. What one insight from 28:1-31:9 would you like to concentrate on during the coming week?

_____

_____

_____

_____

_____

10. How would you like this truth to affect your life? How do you fall short or need to grow in this area?

_____

_____

_____

_____

_____

11. What steps do you plan to take to begin making this truth a part of your habits and attitudes?

_____

_____

_____

_____

_____

12. List any questions you have about 28:1-31:9.

_____

_____

_____

_____

For the group

Warm-up. Ask group members what conditions in their world tempt them to grow anxious, to feel unrestful, to seek, perhaps frantically, for solutions or escapes. Such conditions may be the national economy, personal finances, instability at work, family strife, and so on.

Then set the scene in Isaiah 28-31 for the group—the struggle to make ends meet; the fear of war; a jaded, worldly wise, pleasure-loving government. The king loves God but has been convinced that military might and political independence will glorify God more than moral purity under Assyrian oppression. How does Judah's situation resemble your own? How are your anxieties like and unlike Judah's?

Read aloud. Choose a short piece of these chapters to read, such as 30:15-18. This will help set the mood of the passage without taking too much time.

Summarize. At this point the group may have only a vague impression of what Isaiah is saying, but try to draw out some basic points. For instance, how does "woe" characterize his message? What does he talk about—Egypt, God's Word, national security, a cornerstone, a measuring line, justice, wickedness, rest.

Questions. These chapters are not easy to follow. They may well be composed of many short prophecies that Isaiah spoke at various times during a year or more of debate about Egypt. Young's and Kidner's commentaries both do good jobs of explaining Isaiah's train of thought.

Still, the basic point of the section is clear enough: Samaria has sinned and will be destroyed (28:1-4), but a remnant will survive (28:5-6); however, the remnant in Judah is almost as bad and will also suffer (28:7-31:3). Your task is to see what Judah's leaders and people were doing wrong, what God expected, how He planned to deal with the sin, and how this message applies to you. As so often in Isaiah, the central issue is obedient trust.

Summarize. What basic message is Isaiah trying to get across in these chapters, and how does it fit into his overall ministry?

For Thought and Discussion: What three (or more) main ideas have you seen developed in chapters 1-35 of Isaiah? What would you say are the primary things the Lord has been trying to get across?

119

Wrap-up.

Worship. Thank God for being in control when political and economic conditions tempt us fearfully to seek other sources of help. Meditate together on the rest He provides to those who trust in Him.

1. *The NIV Study Bible*, page 1054.
2. Kidner, page 606.
3. Kidner, page 606.
4. Kidner, page 606; *The NIV Study Bible*, page 1054.
5. Leupold, volume 1, page 452; Kidner, page 606; *The NIV Study Bible*, page 1055; for other possible meanings of Ariel, see Young, volume 2, pages 304-307.
6. Young, volume 2, page 286; Kidner, page 606.

ISAIAH 36:1-39:8

Crises in Jerusalem

Chapters 36-39 form a bridge between the first and second parts of Isaiah's book. These events fulfill many of Isaiah's predictions in chapters 1-35. At the same time, they foreshadow the exile in Babylon that is the background of chapters 40-66.

In 36:1-37:38 Isaiah recounts Assyria's siege of Jerusalem in 701 BC, a crisis the prophet has been promising for years. In 38:1-39:8 Isaiah describes events that occurred between 705 and 702 BC; they were chronologically earlier than the siege, but the mention of Babylon prepares us for chapter 40.

In 36:1-39:8 observe how men respond to desperate situations and how God maintains control through everything.

For Further Study:
Second Kings 18:1-12 and 2 Chronicles 29:1-31:21 tell some of what Hezekiah did before Sennacherib attacked Judah. Second Kings 18:13-16 and 2 Chronicles 32:1-23 add information about Sennacherib's invasion. Second Chronicles 32:24-33 adds to Isaiah 38:1-39:8.

Sennacherib's attack (36:1-37:38)

Isaiah's efforts to persuade Hezekiah not to ally with Egypt were in vain; in 701 BC Hezekiah stopped paying tribute to Assyria and declared Judah's independence. In response, King Sennacherib of Assyria marched the strongest army in the world to overrun his rebel subjects. In a matter of months he took 46 of Judah's walled cities and 200,150 captives.[1] While Sennacherib was besieging the city of Lachish, thirty miles southwest of Jerusalem, he sent a large contingent to Jerusalem to begin a psychological attack on the capital (36:1-2). Isaiah 36:1-37:38 tells how the people of Jerusalem responded to this threat of slow death or exile.

121

For Thought and Discussion: a. What reasons does the commander give for not depending on strategy, military strength, and Egypt's help (36:6,9)?

b. To what extent would Isaiah agree with these reasons (recall chapters 30-31)?

c. How would you respond to the commander's warnings about trusting in military strength? Do your conclusions suggest any applications in your day? If so, what are they?

Field commander (36:2,4). The Assyrian title *Rab-shakeh* (NASB, KJV) denotes a military official of some kind.[2]

High places (36:7). Hezekiah destroyed the many shrines where the people worshiped Baal and insisted that Judah make sacrifices only in Jerusalem (2 Kings 18:4).

The LORD . . . told me (36:10). Spies may have informed Sennacherib of Isaiah's prophecies, and the Assyrian commander was twisting the prophet's words.

Aramaic (36:11). The diplomatic language used throughout the Near East at that time. The common people of Judah spoke only Hebrew, but the officials all knew Aramaic also. The Assyrian commander wanted to incite fear and disloyalty among the common soldiers.

1. The central question of the commander's tempting speech is in 36:4-5—"On what are you basing this confidence of yours? . . . On whom are you depending. . . ?" What reasons does he give for trusting the king of Assyria rather than depending on the Lord (36:7-10,14-20)?

_____

_____

_____

_____

_____

_____

_____

2. How would you refute the commander's arguments?

_____

_____

_____

_____

_____

_____

Optional Application: Have you ever been tempted and threatened as the field commander tempted Jerusalem's people? How should we deal with this kind of temptation?

Clothes torn . . . sackcloth (36:22-37:2). Tearing one's clothes was a sign of great emotion, such as mourning or horror at blasphemy. Sackcloth was a rough, uncomfortable fabric worn as a sign of grief or humility.

3. a. How do the people respond to the commander's threats and promises (36:21-22)?

_____

_____

_____

  b. Why is or isn't this a good way to respond to this kind of temptation?

_____

_____

_____

_____

_____

4. a. Write down each thing Hezekiah does when he hears the Assyrian's message (37:1-4).

_____

_____

_____

_____

123

For Thought and Discussion: Compare how Hezekiah responds to invasion and illness in 36:1-38:22 to how his father Ahaz responded to danger in 7:1-12. What lessons can we draw from this contrast?

For Thought and Discussion: What can we learn about prayer from 37:14-20?

b. Why are Hezekiah's actions a godly response to this crisis? (Consider: What attitudes lie behind his actions?)

_____

_____

_____

_____

_____

5. How does the Lord answer Hezekiah's plea (37:5-8)?

_____

_____

_____

_____

6. When he hears that Egypt is marching to aid Judah, Sennacherib sends another message to Hezekiah (37:9-13) like the one he sent before (36:18-20). What does Hezekiah do about this message (37:14-20)?

_____

_____

_____

_____

Cherubim (37:16). A kind of angel. In the holiest part of the Temple stood the ark of the covenant, a wooden chest containing the Ten Commandments and other signs of God's deeds. The golden lid of the ark was called the atonement cover ("mercy seat" in KJV), and on each end of the cover was a golden cherub with its wings spread over the ark. In the space above the atonement cover and between the cherubim, God localized His presence among His people.

124

Therefore, the atonement cover was regarded as God's throne.[3]

---

7. From 37:15-20, describe what Hezekiah believes about God.

_____

_____

_____

_____

_____

_____

This year . . . (37:30). Sennacherib had attacked in about March of 701 BC, the time of harvest, and he had destroyed or confiscated that year's produce. Therefore, the people could only eat what grew from the seeds of harvested grain that happened to sprout. Sennacherib was not going to leave until after October of 701, when the next year's harvest should be planted. So, the people were going to have to eat chance sproutings in 700 also. But they would be able to plant in October of 700 and harvest in March of 699.[4]

Angel of the LORD (37:36). The Lord's angel (the Hebrew word means "messenger") struck down all the firstborn in Egypt in like manner (Exodus 12:12). The Greek historian Herodotus recorded that Sennacherib's army was destroyed by a sudden onslaught of bubonic plague,[5] but we need not look for a natural disease that could kill so many people overnight.[6]

Soon after the plague, Sennacherib received word of revolt in Babylon, and he withdrew north to quell it.

One day (37:38). In 681 BC, Sennacherib was assassinated by two of his sons.[7] Isaiah probably wrote down the prophecies he gave in 701 BC almost immediately, but 37:38 shows that he

Optional Application: Think about 37:14-20. In what ways does your prayer life reflect your convictions about God? In what ways doesn't it? How can you increasingly incorporate your beliefs into your prayers as Hezekiah does?

For Thought and Discussion: a. The Lord's answer to Hezekiah's prayer is a prophecy against Sennacherib and a promise for Hezekiah (37:21-35). What does the Lord say?
b. What does this tell you about God's character?
c. How does this prophecy reflect the themes of Isaiah's message as a whole?

For Thought and Discussion: Compare what happened to Hezekiah in his Temple (37:14-35) to what happened to Sennacherib in his (37:38). What can we learn from this?

For Thought and Discussion: The Lord responded favorably to Hezekiah's prayer (38:3-8). What do you think of Hezekiah's prayer? In what ways is or isn't it a model for us, and why? Could you honestly say what Hezekiah did in 38:3?

For Further Study: Hezekiah's hymn (38:9-20) is fine poetry, expressing the emotions of a terminally ill man of faith. What did Hezekiah believe and feel about God, life, and death?

Optional Application: How are Hezekiah's prayers (37:14-20; 38:3,9-20) relevant to your life? How could you act and pray with the same attitudes? Consider meditating on these prayers during the next week.

recorded the narrative parts of 36:1-37:38 after the assassination in 681.

---

8. Is Hezekiah's example relevant to your life? If so, how? (Also, is there any specific action you would like to take in order to apply it?)

_____

_____

_____

_____

_____

_____

Hezekiah's illness (38:1-22)

Hezekiah fell ill in 703 or 702 BC, about a year before Sennacherib invaded Judah. Egypt (31:1, 36:6, 37:9) and Babylon (39:1) were both planning revolts against Assyria, and factions in Jerusalem were urging Hezekiah to join with them.

9. What good examples does Hezekiah set for an ill or healed person in 38:3,9-20?

_____

_____

_____

_____

_____

_____

_____

126

Sign (38:7). It seems that the Lord commonly affirmed Isaiah's words by signs (7:11,14), although He did not do this with all His prophets. There have been many explanations of exactly what the Lord did to move the shadow.

A poultice of figs (38:21). A fig paste applied to the boils and left to dry was the standard medical treatment for this ailment. Modern doctors doubt its usefulness, but the Lord empowered the poultice in Hezekiah's case at least.

For Thought and Discussion: How do you interpret Hezekiah's attitude in 39:8?

For Thought and Discussion: Why is 39:1-8 important in Isaiah's book? What does it show about God?

Babylon foreseen (39:1-8)

Merodach-Baladan reigned in Babylon from 721 to 710 BC, when Assyria forced him to submit. He revolted in 705, but Sennacherib sent him fleeing in 703. Apparently, Merodach-Baladan seized the opportunity of Hezekiah's recovery to send envoys to Jerusalem in 702. Their real errand was probably to urge Hezekiah to rebel against Assyria, which Hezekiah did shortly thereafter. According to 2 Chronicles 32:24-31, Hezekiah revealed ungodly pride in showing off to the Babylonians.

For Isaiah, it was not bad enough that Hezekiah was lending attentive ears to the conspirators. Worse still, the Lord revealed to him that the descendants of these Babylonians would depopulate Judah a century later.

Rooted in history, chapter 39 confirms that the Lord revealed the Babylonian exile to Isaiah. When Isaiah retired from political involvement sometime after 701 BC, the Lord comforted him with what lay beyond the exile—the revelations of chapters 40-66.

Your response

10. If you haven't already planned an application in question 8, is there an insight from 36:1-39:8 that you would like to act upon? If so, what is that insight?

_____

_____

_____

_____

_____

11. How does this insight apply to you?

_____

_____

_____

_____

12. What prayer and/or action can you pursue to
    begin putting this insight into practice?

_____

_____

_____

_____

_____

_____

13. List any questions you have about 36:1-39:8.

_____

_____

_____

For the group

Warm-up. The theme of trust has been recurring for
several weeks now. Ask the group whether anyone
has had opportunities to apply this kind of trust
during the past few weeks.

Read aloud. You may want to read short pieces of
each section (36:1-37:38, 38:1-22, and 39:1-8) as
you come to it, so that you have less to listen to at
once.

Summarize. Have someone briefly retell what happens in each of the three narratives, and what the main purpose or message of each seems to be.

Hezekiah's illness. Critics love to debunk this story, claiming that both the sun's retreat and the healing through a fig poultice are impossible. However, problems dissolve once we grant the Lord's ability to do whatever He wants through the laws of physics and chemistry that He devised.

For us, the story's importance is what it shows about prayer and God's sovereignty.

Babylon foreseen. In the interest of time, we have made questions about this passage optional. You might briefly ask what happens in 39:1-8 and why it is important for Isaiah's message as a whole.

Summarize. We called chapters 1-39 "The Book of Judgment." What would you call it? What is it about? What main ideas run through it? In what three or four ways is it most relevant to your lives? How has studying it affected the ways you think and act?

Wrap-up. This logical break in the book is a good time for another evaluation. Ask the group what they liked best about this meeting, what they liked least, and how they would change the study in future.

Consider putting Isaiah aside for a week or two to concentrate on prayer, fellowship, or something else. Even a good study can begin to wear after eleven weeks. However, don't break for so long that you forget chapters 1-39, for they are tied to 40-66.

Worship.

1. William Sanford La Sor, "2 Kings," *The New Bible Commentary: Revised*, page 362.
2. Young, volume 2, page 458.
3. *The NIV Study Bible*, page 123.
4. *The NIV Study Bible*, page 563.
5. *The NIV Study Bible*, page 1069.
6. Young, volume 2, page 505.
7. *The NIV Study Bible*, page 1069. La Sor says 682, but the Assyrian year overlaps our calendar, so either year is possible.

ISAIAH 40:1-48:22

The Only God

In 1:1-39:8 the dominant note was judgment, but in 40:1-66:24 the dominant note is "comfort" (40:1). The former section ended in 701 BC with the Assyrian storm over and the cloud of Babylon only beginning to gather on the horizon. Between 39:8 and 40:1 lay 160 years of moral decay, political collapse, the siege and destruction of Jerusalem, wholesale slaughter, deportation to forced labor, and fruitless longing for the land of promise. Through this gathering darkness Isaiah's vision pierces, falling upon the year 538 BC when Cyrus of Persia has vanquished the Babylonian army and declared that all deported peoples may return to their homes and their gods (see page 139).

The events Isaiah describes in 40:1-66:24 are from 538 BC and the even further future, but his point of view remains in the early years of the 600s. A theme of these chapters is that the Lord is announcing His saving acts *long before* they take place, so that all the world will know that "apart from me there is no God" (44:6).

The lessons that follow will give you only a taste of these rich chapters. Isaiah interweaves his themes in masterful counterpoint, but for simplicity we will trace the logic of the whole message rather than studying it passage by passage. Of Isaiah's many themes, we will focus on these:

- the Lord's greatness;
- Israel's status as *chosen* and mission as *servant*;

For Further Study:
Isaiah spoke in part
to encourage the
exiles in Babylon. Why
should they trust the
Lord's promises of
40:1-11 in spite of
Babylon's apparent
might (40:6-8)?

For Further Study:
a. How did John the
Baptist tell people to
prepare the way for
the Lord (Luke
3:4-18)?
   b. How does this
apply to you?

- Israel's failure, and the resulting need for a true Servant;
- the glorious future of God's people and the dreadful future of the wicked.

To introduce you to the flavor of the section, this lesson will take you swiftly through the first nine chapters, looking at God. If this is the first time you have studied these chapters, don't try to absorb every detail, and don't worry if the train of thought is sometimes unclear. Instead, try to let the character of God overwhelm you and alter your perspective on the world. Observe as much as you can, but feel free to dwell on just a few of the many passages. Any of them would be excellent for meditation. There is nothing wrong with spending a lot of time thinking about one or two passages in each question, since the passages tend to repeat and reinforce each other.

It would be a good idea to read at least 40:1-48:22 at one sitting before you start on these questions. The outline on page 19 may help you orient yourself. If you find it more helpful to outline the book for yourself, sketch an outline of 40:1-48:22.

Voice (40:3). The Lord begins chapter 40 by declaring that His people have served their sentence in Babylon and will now be brought home. A herald goes before the returning procession in the oriental manner, announcing that a king is coming and commanding that a suitable road be made for a royal advent.

---

1. In chapters 40-48, the Lord addresses both Israel and the pagan nations. Of what key truth is He trying to convince them (43:11; 44:6; 45:5-7,18; 48:12)?

   _____

   _____

   _____

2. Why does the Lord so strongly want Israel and the nations to grasp this truth?

132

Israel (41:13-14, 48:17-19) _____

_____

_____

_____

the nations (45:22-24) _____

_____

_____

_____

Lebanon (40:16). Not even the famous huge cedars of Lebanon could feed enough altar fires to fully honor the Lord. Nor could that country's abundant wildlife provide enough offerings.

Be silent (41:1). Like a Near Eastern overlord, God calls the nations into His courtroom to prove why He is unworthy of worship. (See 41:21-29.)

One from the east (41:2). Cyrus, the Persian king who was going to overthrow Babylon in 539 BC. Cyrus was equally "from the north" (41:25).

---

3. Both Israel and the nations are inclined to think the Lord is no greater than the pagan nations and their idols. After all, it appears that Assyria and Babylon have subdued Israel by the might of their gods.

   How does the Lord counter this belief that the nations and their idols are as great as He?

   40:6-8 _____

   _____

   _____

   _____

   40:12-17 _____

   _____

For Thought and Discussion: God's lordship was on trial in Isaiah's day. Is this true in your day? If so, how? How would you refute those who challenge God's right or ability to run the world?

For Thought and Discussion: Why did God name Cyrus more than a hundred years before Cyrus was born?

Optional Application: Do you worship anything manmade (44:12-20)? If so, what?

Optional Application: Which of the statements the Lord makes about Himself in question 3 are especially relevant to your situation? How should you respond?

40:18-26 _____

41:1-4 _____

41:21-29, 44:28-45:7, 48:14-15 _____

43:14-21 _____

44:12-20 _____

44:24-26 _____

_____

_____

_____

_____

_____

**Optional
Application:** Read
41:14; 43:3,14; 44:6.
How is it important in
your life that the Lord
is your Redeemer, the
Holy One of Israel,
your King? Meditate
on these titles, and
think of some ways to
respond in prayer and
action.

**For Thought and
Discussion:** a. In
what sense does God
"create disaster"
(45:7)?
b. In what sense
is He "a God who
hides himself"
(45:15)?

Redeemer (41:14). The Hebrew word *go'el* names a
kinsman who frees or aids a family member. He
might pay off his family's debts, buy back family
land that has been sold to cover debts, or buy
back a family member who has been sold for
debt (Leviticus 25:23-55). If a family member is
enslaved by an enemy, the kinsman-redeemer
liberates him in battle (Genesis 14:1-16).[1] The
Lord is Israel's Family Protector, recovering the
people's land and liberty.

Egypt . . . Cush . . . Seba (43:3). At the same time
that Cyrus the Persian was freeing the Jews
from Babylon and returning them to Judah, he
was conquering Egypt, Cush, and Seba (see the
map on page 9).

A way through the sea (43:16). When the Israelites
came to the Red Sea as they fled from Egypt,
God parted the waters so that His people could
pass. Then, when the Egyptian soldiers tried to
pursue the Israelites, God closed the waters over
the soldiers (Exodus 14:21-31). Isaiah repeatedly compares the deliverance from Babylon to
the exodus from Egypt.

Secret (45:19). Although God "hides himself"
(45:15) in certain ways, He is not like the spirits
whom mediums summon with arcane rites in
clandestine places. He proclaims His plans
openly through His prophets, and anyone may
seek Him frankly.

135

Optional Application: Have you ever been tempted to question God's methods, motives, or abilities? If so, how is 45:9-13 relevant?

For Thought and Discussion: Why is it important that the Lord is not just God of one part of the human race or of just the earth?

Optional Application: Why is it important for you personally to know that the Lord . . .
is the Creator of the Universe?
carries out plans laid long ago?
is the Redeemer of His people?
is greater than the nations and their gods?

4. The Lord stresses that He is predicting what He will do 160 years later in Cyrus' time (45:19-21). Why is it important (for the faithful exiles and for us) that the Lord can predict His plans through the prophets and then carry them out? (*Optional:* See 41:14, 48:1-7.)

_____

_____

_____

_____

_____

_____

5. The Lord also emphasizes that He is the Creator of Israel and the whole universe. Why is this fact important for us to remember? What are its implications for us?

40:12-14 _____

_____

_____

_____

40:25-31 _____

_____

_____

_____

_____

45:9-13 _____

_____

_____

_____

_____

_____

136

Bel . . . Nebo (46:1). Gods of Babylon. Their huge idols were carried through the streets of Babylon on festival days, but in 46:1-2 Isaiah portrays them as toppling and overburdening those who bear them into exile.[2]

Sit in the dust (47:1). Chapter 47 is set in the rhythm of a Hebrew dirge. Sitting in the dust was a sign of mourning. Grinding grain and washing laundry in the streams were menial tasks.[3]

I am (47:8). Babylon's boasts in 47:7-8 are virtually claims to deity.

Magic . . . astrologers (47:12-13). Because the floods and droughts of the Euphrates River were capricious and dangerous, the Babylonians had long seen life as uncertain. To grasp some sense of control, they zealously pursued magic and invented astrology. They theorized that the movements of heavenly bodies somehow affect events on earth, and therefore one could predict events by observing the heavens. The theory was never proven, but the Babylonians built their culture around it and devoted far more energy to it than any other nation.[4]

6. Chose one or two of the passages you have observed in questions 1-5. Meditate on them for awhile, and write down how they encourage, exhort, or warn you. How should these insights affect your actions and attitudes this week?

_____

_____

_____

_____

_____

_____

Optional Application: Do you believe that 40:29-31 applies to you? How does the rest of chapters 40-48 help convince you of this fact? How should fully believing these truths affect your actions this week?

Optional Application: Are you at all like Israel as described in 48:1-6? If so, how? What can you do about this?

For Further Study: Go back through chapters 40-48 listing observations about the Lord and how they are relevant to you. For instance, consider 40:11.

Optional Application: Does the Lord do for you what He claims in 48:17-18? How can you let Him do this?

7. If you have any questions about 40:1-48:22, list
them here.

_____

_____

_____

For the group

Warm-up. Before you turn to your study guides, ask
the group what attribute of God each person has experienced most vividly today. Some people may feel
that they experienced many aspects of God today.
Others may have felt distant from God. This is an acceptable answer, but the group should plan to encourage that person in prayer at the end of your meeting.

Read aloud. To remind the group of Isaiah's tone of
voice and his themes, read 40:1-31.

Summarize. Give the group a few minutes to leaf
through the chapters. Then ask several people to
tell what Isaiah says in general. You may not come
up with a clear single focus, but threads like comfort, debunking idols, and asserting God's fore-
knowledge should be a starting point.

Questions. You may need to have someone explain
the courtroom scene in these chapters. The Lord
calls His accusers to testify against Him, then re-
futes their charges. What are the charges, and how
does God refute them? Don't try to discuss every
verse listed in the questions. Instead, let each person share how some verses are especially significant
to him or her. Be open about what is really happening in your lives.

Wrap-up. Encourage each person to choose one
short passage and meditate on it during the coming
week. You could plan to come next week ready to
share how you've experienced that aspect of God or
how recalling that aspect has affected your response
to some situation.

Lesson thirteen will cover some of the passages
in 40:1-48:22 from another point of view. The focus
there will be on Israel.

138

Worship. Praise God for His character and attributes that you have observed.

The Exile, part one

King Nebuchadnezzar had scarcely finished conquering Assyria's empire for Babylon when the little king of Judah rebelled against his new master. Like Sennacherib a century earlier, Nebuchadnezzar struck harshly. He besieged Jerusalem in 605 BC, took many of the vessels from God's Temple, and carried off most of Judah's young royal and noble men. Among them was the prophet Daniel (Daniel 1:1-3).

Nebuchadnezzar followed with another siege and deportation in 597. Ten thousand men—the rest of the royalty, nobility, smiths, craftsmen, and soldiers—followed Nebuchadnezzar into slavery in the cities and farms of Babylon. Among them was the prophet Ezekiel.

But Judah's new king Zedekiah had not learned God's message to Ahaz, to Hezekiah, and to his own brother and nephew (who had been kings in 605 and 597). In his own way, the prophet Jeremiah tried to tell Zedekiah "the LORD is salvation," but Zedekiah ignored him. Zedekiah allied with Egypt against Babylon, and this time Nebuchadnezzar had Jerusalem looted, burned, and demolished. Only about half of Judah's population remained to till the land after the Babylonians killed or deported the rest.

(continued on page 149)

---

1. de Vaux, pages 21-22.
2. Kidner, page 615.
3. *The NIV Study Bible*, page 1085.
4. Stephen F. Mason, *A History of the Sciences* (New York: Collier Books, 1962), pages 15-21.

LESSON THIRTEEN

ISAIAH 41:8-16, 42:1-25, 43:8-24, 48:1-6, 56:9-57:13, 58:1-59:20

Israel's Calling

Only a remnant of Israel survived Assyria and Babylon. Exiles they might be, dispersed throughout the Near East, but they remained the heirs of the covenant with Abraham. God had a plan for the people He had freed from Egypt, guided to the promised land, and protected for centuries. He had given this people His Law and revealed Himself to them for a purpose.

Israel's mission is a theme of Isaiah's book and a key to the New Testament. What had God intended for Israel, and how well had the nation fulfilled its calling?

If you've never read Isaiah 49-66, it would be a good idea to do so. However, if your time is limited, you can read just the passages in this lesson. The outline on pages 19-20 may help you see individual passages in context.

Mission (41:8-16, 42:1-9)

1. What did the Lord want all nations to know about Him and to do about that knowledge? (Recall 45:22 and what you learned in lesson twelve.)

_____

_____

_____

For Thought and Discussion: Consider Genesis 12:1-3 and Isaiah 42:6. What do you learn about God from His desire to send Israel to the nations?

141

Optional Application: How do you know that God has chosen, redeemed, and promised to protect you? How do you know His promises in Isaiah apply to you (Galatians 3:7-9, Romans 4:13-25)? Meditate on these facts from 41:8-14, 43:1-7.

For Thought and Discussion: How are 41:8-14 and 43:1-7 a motivation for fulfilling the mission in 42:1-9?

For Thought and Discussion: How could Israel have been a "light for the Gentiles" (42:6)?

Servant (41:8). "In the royal terminology of the ancient Near East 'servant' meant something like 'trusted envoy' or 'confidential representative.'"[1]

The servant's identity is ambiguous in Isaiah. In 41:8-9 and 44:21 the nation Israel is clearly the servant. But 42:1-9, 49:1-7, 50:4-11, and 52:13-53:12 suggest a person who will fulfill the servant's mission. Passages like 42:18-22 are uncertain—is this Israel who is deaf, blind, ignorant, and plundered? Or, is this the Lord's Representative, the Messiah?

Threshing sledge (41:15). To separate grain from stalks, farmers drove wooden sledges fitted with sharp teeth over the cut stalks.

2. Read 41:8-16. What words and phrases did the Lord use to describe Israel and its relationship to Him (41:8-9,14)?

_____

_____

_____

_____

_____

3. What did the Lord promise to do for Israel (41:10-14)?

_____

_____

_____

_____

_____

4. If Israel was going to be God's servant, what tasks would Israel have to fulfill (42:1,6-7; 43:10-13)?

_____

_____

_____

_____

_____

_____

**For Thought and
Discussion:** How
was Israel's *history* a
witness to God's sov-
ereignty even though
Israel's *behavior* was
a poor witness
(43:12-21)? (The
books of Exodus
through 2 Kings will
answer this question.)

Witnesses (43:9-10,12). In 41:1-29, Isaiah records a
court case between the Lord and the nations
who refuse to acknowledge His sovereignty. In
43:8-13 is another piece of this trial. The Lord
commands the nations to bring their witnesses
to prove that other gods exist (43:8-9), and He
summons Israel as His witness (43:10-13). Israel
says nothing to defend the Lord, but He points
to the ways He has "revealed and saved and
proclaimed" (43:12) as evidence for His
supremacy.

For Further Study:
Jesus and Paul enu-
merate Israel's fail-
ures in Luke
11:37-52 and
Romans 9:30-10:4.

Failure (42:18-25; 43:8-13,22-24; 48:1-6; 56:9-57:13; 58:1-59:20)

5. a. How does the Lord describe Israel's effective-
ness as God's servant and messenger to the
nations (42:18-19,22)? (*Optional:* See also
6:9-10, 26:18.)

_____

_____

_____

b. Why is Israel ineffective (42:20-25)?
(*Optional:* Compare Romans 2:17-24.)

_____

_____

_____

143

For Thought and Discussion: Do you weary yourself for the Lord, or do you weary Him (43:22-24)?

For Thought and Discussion: What does it mean to "invoke the God of Israel—but not in truth or righteousness" (48:1)?

For Thought and Discussion: Why did Israel refuse to acknowledge that God controlled what happened (48:3-6)?

For Thought and Discussion: a. The people tried to solve their problems with idolatry and magic (57:1-9). How did they react when that attempt failed (57:10)?
    b. Do modern people ever react similarly to failures? Explain.

6. Throughout the prophecies in chapters 40-66, the Lord reminds Israel how poor a servant and witness the nation has been. Look at the following passages, and summarize what the people are doing wrong in each case.

43:22-24 (observe the repeated words "wearied" and "burdened")

_____

_____

_____

_____

48:1-2 _____

_____

_____

_____

48:3-6 _____

_____

_____

_____

___

Watchmen . . . shepherds (56:10-11). In 56:9-12, the Lord invites invaders ("beasts") to devour the sheep of Israel because the leaders ("watchmen," "dogs," "shepherds") are interested only in sleep, food, and drink.

Sorceress . . . adulterers (57:3). In 57:1-13, the Lord condemns what the people do when the leaders abandon their responsibility. Idolatry is the literal offense; the Lord likens it to adultery against Israel's true husband, Himself.

Sacrifices and ritual sex acts were commonly performed under sacred trees (57:5) and on hilltops (57:7). People sacrificed children and offered perfumed oils to the god Molech (57:5,9). King Manasseh sacrificed his own son

144

to Molech around the time Isaiah was writing these passages (2 Kings 21:1-6). It was the nation's obstinate rebellion under Manasseh that moved the Lord to let Babylon devastate Judah (2 Kings 21:10-15).

7. Summarize the people's sins described in these passages also.

a. How had Israel corrupted the disciplines of prayer, fasting, and humility (58:1-10,13)?

_____

_____

_____

_____

_____

_____

b. What kinds of sin are most prominent in 59:3-15?

_____

_____

_____

_____

For Thought and Discussion: a. Why is 58:3 a poor attitude with which to approach God in prayer?

b. Why is 58:6-7 a better preparation for prayer? How can you apply this in your own life?

For Thought and Discussion: a. Why does sin hinder God from intervening to save people (59:1-2)?

b. Why does God not listen to self-centered prayer (58:3,13)?

c. Why does the Lord so detest lying (59:1-16)?

8. The Lord reminded Israel of all these sins for at least three reasons: to explain why He was going to let Babylon devastate Judah; to move the survivors to repentance; and to demonstrate that Israel had failed to fulfill its mission. But Israel's failure was not the end of God's plan. To prove His sovereignty to the nations (44:6-8) and to stubborn Israel (48:3-11), He announced His solution ahead of time.

What was God's solution to Israel's failure (59:15-20)?

_____

_____

For Thought and
Discussion: a. How
is the Church's mis-
sion different from
Israel's?

b. What power to
fulfill our mission do
we have that Israel
did not (Acts 1:8;
Romans 8:1-17,
26-27)? How can we
avoid neglecting that
power?

Optional
Application: If one of
the passages in ques-
tion 5, 6, or 7 convicts
you of sin, plan to
reread it each day for
the next week. Con-
fess your sin to God,
and ask Him to en-
able you to think and
act differently. Seek
ways of practicing the
right actions you think
you should follow.
Writing a list of pos-
sible ways may help
you to remember
them.

_____

_____

_____

Lessons fourteen and fifteen will give you a
chance to explore this solution further.

Your response

9. In what ways is God's mission for the Church
like the mission He gave Israel? (*Optional:*
Compare your answers in questions 1 and 4 to
Matthew 5:13-16, 28:18-20; John 13:34-35; Acts
1:8; Ephesians 1:3-12, 4:1.)

_____

_____

_____

_____

_____

10. a. In which aspect of your mission would you
most like to grow?

_____

_____

b. Is there anything you can do to pursue
growth in this area? If so, what? (Consider
the "Optional Applications" in this lesson.)

_____

_____

_____

_____

_____

11. This lesson skimmed the surface of a deep
subject. Try to summarize the most important
things you have learned.

146

_____

_____

_____

_____

_____

_____

12. List any questions you have about the passages in this lesson. Also, if you would like to delve more deeply into one of the topics or passages, write down your questions or interests.

_____

_____

_____

_____

Optional Application: Each day for the next week, ask God to show you one situation in which you can act in accord with your calling. Ask Him to enable you to fulfill your mission. If you feel guilty about not being a perfect servant, confess your feelings and ask God to help you let go of guilt.

For the group

In order to keep this study as brief as possible, we've made a lot of questions optional in this lesson. If you have time, you can certainly take several meetings to cover these passages more carefully and answer the optional questions in separate notebooks.

Warm-up. Let anyone who wants to do so share how meditating on last week's passages affected his or her life during the past week.

Ask the group what comes to mind when you think of yourselves as God's "servants." What does this mean in your lives?

Read aloud. Perhaps 41:8-16 will set the tone of the lesson.

Summarize. What is the lesson about? The title "Israel's Calling" and the subtitles "Mission" and "Failure" should be clues.

Questions. Discuss *calling* and *chosenness* before

you plunge into *mission* and *failure*. The loving, chosen relationship of 41:8-14 and 43:1-7 is the reason and motivation for the mission of 42:1-9.

If your group knows the New Testament, someone may complain that 42:1-9,18-19 is about Christ, not Israel. If so, point out that in 49:3,5 the servant is called Israel but also has a mission to Israel. In lesson fourteen you'll see that Christ fulfills the mission God gave Israel because Israel was unable to do so. Israel was meant to be a light and a blessing to the nations (Genesis 12:3, Isaiah 42:6), but Christ became the true Israel who accomplished this task. As 59:15-20 reveals (question 8), God Himself (in Christ) had to do what Israel failed to do.

It would be profitable, but time-consuming, to spend a lot of time on the sins in questions 6 and 7. You could comb through each passage, asking what sins God is condemning and how a modern person might commit similar ones. You will have to decide whether to take the time to let God convict you through a detailed study of these passages, or whether to let them build for you a picture of rebellion against a calling.

Questions 9 and 10 treat application positively, asking you to identify with Israel's mission. Let the group discuss how they can fulfill their mission in the power of God's Spirit, since Israel failed by rejecting God's power. Try to discuss not just the Christian mission in general terms, but the group members' missions in specific terms in the present.

Several of the optional questions ask you to identify with and repent from Israel's failures. You will need to discuss whether, and how strongly, to urge the group to examine their own attitudes about prayer, worship, and loving obedience in light of these passages. Repenting of attitudes that block God's enablement can be a crucial part of fulfilling our mission.

Summarize. Summarize Israel's calling and how the people fell short. Also, summarize your intended applications, whether focused on mission or repentance.

Wrap-up. Remind the group that the next few lessons will examine God's solution to Israel's failure.

Worship. Thank God for calling and choosing you,

for sending you with a mission, and for equipping you with His Spirit to fulfill it. Praise Him for His wise plan for the world and His unwillingness to abandon the nations without a light.

The Exile, part two

The book of Lamentations contains five poems of Jerusalem's fall by an eyewitness. Psalm 137 is a memory of the grief of exile. We know little of the exiles' lives, except that they were captives in a rough, idolatrous, alien nation that despised them. They survived by clinging to each other, to God's Law, and to the words they had received from prophets like Isaiah.

For God had not sent them comfortless into exile. The prophets gave meaning to the past by explaining that the captivity was payment for gross sin. They gave hope to the future by promising that the captivity was temporary; after seventy years God would lead a remnant home (Isaiah 10:20-22, Jeremiah 25:11-12). Finally, the Law gave purpose to the present by showing the people how to live rightly before God each day.

(continued on page 157)

---

1. *The NIV Study Bible*, page 1074; Young, volume 3, pages 80-81.

ISAIAH 42:1-9, 49:1-7, 50:4-11

The Servant: 1

God had called Israel to be His servant, but Israel had rebelled against its calling. So, God said that since there was no one else, He would Himself intervene to accomplish His aims (59:15-20). The way He planned to intervene was to call another Servant to fulfill His desires for the world.

It is not always clear in Isaiah's prophecies when the Lord is speaking of the nation Israel as His servant and when He is speaking of this other Servant, so for centuries the full significance of the "Servant Songs" was a mystery to the Jews. Try to feel the mystery the Jews felt, even as you read in the light of the New Testament.

Bruised reed . . . smoldering wick (42:3). Someone who is weak.

Islands (42:4). To the Jews, the coastlands and islands of the Mediterranean represented the pagan peoples beyond the Near East.

1. Reread 42:1-9. In lesson thirteen you read this as Israel's commission, but now write everything you observe about the true Servant's . . .

   equipment for service (42:1,6) _____

For Thought and Discussion: Why is the Servant's intervention (42:1-9) the same as God's intervention (59:15-20)?

For Further Study: How is Jesus deaf and blind (42:18-19) in a different way than Israel? Compare 6:9-10 to 11:3.

151

For Further Study:
How does Jesus fulfill Isaiah 42, 49, and 50? Study some of the cross-references below, as well as others you may find.

a. How has He been bringing justice to the nations (42:1)? See Matthew 5:21-26, 28:18-20; Acts 1:6-8.

b. How will He bring justice at His second coming? See pages 71-72.

c. How does He not break bruised reeds (42:3)? See Matthew 11:28-29, 12:15-21; Luke 8:43-48; John 4:4-42, 8:3-11.

d. How does He give light to the Gentiles (42:6, 49:6)? See John 8:12; 2 Corinthians 4:4-6; Ephesians 2:11-22, 3:14-21, 5:8-14.

e. How does He open blind eyes and free prisoners (42:7)? See Luke 8:26-39, 13:10-17; John 9:1-41, 12:44-46, 14:8-9; 2 Corinthians 4:4-6.

f. How has He and will He bring Israel back to God (49:5)? See Romans 11:1-32.

character (42:2-4) _____

_____

_____

_____

mission (42:1,4,6-7) _____

_____

_____

_____

_____

2. In what ways does this Servant resemble the Son of David prophesied in 9:6-7 and 11:1-9?

_____

_____

_____

_____

3. In 49:1-5 the Servant speaks about Himself.

a. In what sense is His "mouth like a sharpened sword" (49:2)? (*Optional:* See Ephesians 6:17, Hebrews 4:12, Revelation 1:16.)

_____

_____

_____

_____

b. Is the Servant's task easy and completely joyful? What does He say about this in 49:4?

_____

_____

152

_____

_____

c. How do people respond to the Servant at first (49:7)?

_____

_____

_____

_____

d. The Lord calls His Servant "Israel" in 49:3, yet what is His mission (49:5-6)?

_____

_____

_____

_____

4. Immediately after the Lord laments Israel's sin (50:1-3), the Servant speaks again (50:4-11).

a. What does the Servant say about Himself in 50:4-5?

_____

_____

_____

_____

_____

b. According to 50:6-9, how will the Servant be received when He comes to fulfill His mission?

_____

_____

_____

_____

For Thought and Discussion: How do people's responses to the Servant change, and why (49:5,7)?

For Thought and Discussion: Explain how the Servant both is Israel and has a mission to Israel (49:3,5).

For Thought and Discussion: What attitudes about the Lord and His mission does the Servant show in 50:4-5?

153

Optional Application: Take five minutes to thank Jesus for fulfilling Isaiah's prophecies in your life. Ask Him how He would like you to respond in action to what He has done for you.

c. With what attitudes and actions does the Servant respond to this reception (50:5-9)?

_____

_____

_____

_____

_____

5. Summarize what you have learned about the Servant of the Lord from 42:1-9, 49:1-7, and 50:4-11.

_____

_____

_____

_____

_____

Your response

6. Jesus claimed to be the fulfillment of the Servant prophecies (compare Isaiah 42:1-4 to Matthew 12:18-21). Have you personally experienced Him fulfilling Isaiah 42:1-4,6-7? If so, how?

_____

_____

_____

_____

_____

7. Christians are also God's servants (Luke 16:13). Name at least three ways in which the Servant of the Lord is a model for our actions.

154

_____

_____

_____

_____

_____

_____

_____

8. Consider how Jesus faced opposition as He fulfilled His mission (50:5-9). How should God's people act in light of this example (50:10-11)?

_____

_____

_____

_____

9. Are there any specific ways in which you could act on the deliverance Jesus has wrought (42:6-7) or the example He has set (49:5-6, 50:4-10)? If so, what one or two aspects would you like to concentrate on for the near future?

_____

_____

_____

_____

10. What prayer or other action can you pursue to apply this truth?

_____

_____

_____

_____

_____

_____

11. List any questions you have about this lesson.

_____

_____

_____

_____

_____

For the group

Warm-up. Ask someone to remind the group what God wanted to prove to the nations, how Israel figured into this plan, and how well Israel had succeeded. All this should set the stage for why the true Servant was necessary.

Read aloud.

Summarize. Who is the true Servant, and what do these passages say in general about Him?

Questions. This lesson is fairly straightforward. You will want to bring out the Servant's mission and character, how we can live in light of what He does, and how we can be like Him.

The cross-references that show Jesus' fulfillment of Isaiah's prophecies are important. However, try to spend the major portion of your time discussing how what you know about Jesus affects your lives and how you can act on what you have learned.

Summarize.

Wrap-up.

Worship. Thank God for accomplishing His purposes through His Servant Jesus and His servant the Church. Ask Him how you can participate in fulfilling the Servant's mission.

The Exile, part three

Hope did not disappoint the exiles. In 539 BC, Cyrus of Persia conquered Babylon. His strategy for controlling a vast empire was to win the support of its many peoples rather than to trust sheer force as Assyria and Babylon had done. To achieve this, Cyrus replaced the Babylonian policy of requiring allegiance to Babylonian gods with a policy of religious toleration. Cyrus began to send deported peoples back to their homelands with their confiscated idols. He financed the rebuilding of temples. And he asked his subjects to pray to their own gods for him and his empire.

Whether Cyrus was a sincere universalist or a clever strategist, his policy served the Lord's ends. In 538, Cyrus sent a delegation of Jews to Jerusalem with their temple vessels. He told the Jews to rebuild their Temple and pray for him. Sixty-seven years after the first exiles left Jerusalem, the first group returned.

Naturally, the returnees believed that all of Isaiah's prophecies were coming true. They expected the Messiah to appear at any moment; perhaps their leader Zerubbabel was He! However, it took twenty-two years to overcome local opposition enough to build the Temple. Those Judeans who had not been exiled had assimilated into pagan culture and resented competition for land and power. Harsh weather made crop failures frequent. Squabbles multiplied, while devotion to God waned. The nation remained full of unbelievers and subject to the Persian Empire. The Lord sent prophets (Haggai and Zechariah) and leaders (Ezra and Nehemiah), but although there were periods of repentance and faith, it was soon clear that the return from exile was only a shadow of the true deliverance for which the people must hope. And so they settled down with their Law and their Temple to await the Messiah.

ISAIAH 52:13-53:12

The Servant: 2

Suffering and Glory (52:13-53:12)

From Isaiah 9:1-7, 11:1-16, and 42:1-9, the Jews got the impression that the Messiah would come as a triumphant liberator, a warrior like King David. But already in 49:4,7 and 50:4-9 were disturbing hints that all was not going to be easy and happy for the Servant.

In 52:13-53:12, these hints became blatant. For centuries the religious leaders struggled with the idea that the glorious Messiah was going to suffer, but this prophecy remained a mystery. Even when Jesus came and healed the sick, proclaimed the Kingdom, suffered crucifixion, and rose from the dead, most people refused to believe that an executed criminal was the Savior. The message of the Cross—the message of Isaiah 52:13-53:12—seemed "foolishness" (1 Corinthians 1:18).

Isaiah 52:13-53:12 is a poem. Because it's easy to lose the impact of a passage like this in close analysis, read through the poem meditatively before you begin the questions. Try reading it aloud, expressively and prayerfully, dwelling on phrases that touch you.

For Further Study:
Study the context of the Suffering Servant poem. Consider "Awake, awake!" (52:1), the good news announced in 52:1-12, and especially 52:3,10-12.

Root out of dry ground (53:2). The people of Jesus' day expected the Son of David to be a nobleman, a man of status and imposing appearance. But by that time there had been no true king

For Further Study:
How does Jesus carry
our sins, sicknesses
and sorrows? See
how Matthew 8:16-17
says Christ fulfilled
53:4. See also John
19:17 and 1 Peter
2:24.

For Further Study:
On the sorrows of
Jesus' life, see Mat-
thew 2:13-23; Mark
1:32-34; 3:1-6;
14:32-42,66-72;
15:1-37; Luke
7:11-15;
9:22,41,51-58;
13:34-35; John
11:11-40.

for about six hundred years, and Jesus (the root
and shoot, 11:1,10) was born into an impoverished family of David's line (the dry ground).[1]

1. How did people regard God's Servant when He
came among them (53:2-3)?

_____

_____

_____

_____

_____

Sorrows . . . suffering . . . infirmities (53:3-4).
These Hebrew words can refer to physical or
mental pain, so "griefs" and "sicknesses" are
equally good translations.[2] Scripture regards
mental pain, physical disease, and social ills all
as consequences of the sins of Adam and his
descendents.
    The Hebrew words for "beaten," "injured,"
and "welts" in Isaiah 1:5-6 are the same as the
words for "smitten," "infirmities" and "wounds"
in 53:4-5.[3]

2. According to this poem, the central feature of
the Servant's life was suffering—He was "a man
of sorrows" (53:3). What afflictions did the Servant experience?

53:3 _____

_____

53:4 _____

_____

_____

53:5 _____

_____

_____

53:7-9 _____

_____

_____

_____

For Thought and Discussion: Why did people respond to the Servant as they did (53:2-4)?

3. With what attitude did the Servant undergo His afflictions (53:7)?

_____

_____

_____

_____

4. What did people think when they saw what happened to the Servant (53:4)?

_____

_____

_____

_____

_____

5. However, what was the real purpose of the Servant's suffering and death (53:4-6,10-12)?

_____

_____

_____

_____

_____

_____

Sprinkle (52:15). The priests sprinkled blood or
water on people to cleanse (Leviticus 14:7;
Numbers 8:7, 19:18-19) or consecrate (Exodus
29:21; Leviticus 8:11,30) them.[4]

For our transgressions (53:5). Recall the meaning
of atonement and the atonement cover of the
ark (pages 52 and 124 of this guide). The people
of His generation judged that the Servant was
suffering for His own wrongdoings (53:4), but
in fact He was suffering for ours (53:4-6). The
book of Hebrews explains this in terms of the
atonement sacrifice which was offered yearly to
cover the people's sins (Hebrews 9:1-28).

Each autumn, the high priest would lay
his hands on a live goat and confess over it the
nation's sins. Then the goat would be sent into
the desert to *bear away* the sin. The priest
would also slaughter another goat to *bear the
penalty* for the people's sins. He would sprinkle
the blood on the atonement cover, and then
this goat's body would be burned outside the
city as a sinful thing (Leviticus 16:15-30).

The principle of substitutionary death for
sin was the basis of Israel's sacrificial system.
The Passover lamb was killed annually to
remind the people that God had accepted a substitute for the deaths of all Israel's firstborn in
Egypt (Exodus 12:1-30).

Peace (53:5). "Well-being" in NASB; "that made us
whole" in RSV. Recall from 9:6-7 that the
Hebrew word *shalom* means peace, health,
wholeness, and well-being in all aspects of
life—physical, mental, spiritual, economic,
social, and political. It includes peace between
God and us, made possible because the Servant
has borne the chastisement (punishment for
discipline) earned by our rebellion.[5]

His knowledge (53:11). This phrase is literally, "by
the knowledge of him." It could mean that the
many are justified either because of the Servant's knowledge of God or because of the
many's knowledge of the Servant.

Justify many (53:11). Cause many to be declared
righteous—legally acquitted of wrongdoing

162

because the penalty has been paid. Justification only declares that a person has a new legal standing before God. From then on, the person's moral character should begin to change to fit the new legal status.[6]

6. Explain in your own words what the Servant's death achieves for us.

_____

_____

_____

_____

_____

_____

Grave (53:9). Jesus was crucified between two thieves, as the worst criminal of them all; crucifixion was reserved for the basest criminals. But a rich believer named Joseph gave Jesus his tomb (Matthew 27:38,44,57-60).

7. The Servant would be executed as a criminal and buried (53:8-9). Nevertheless, what else did Isaiah promise would be true of Him (52:13, 53:10-12)?

_____

_____

_____

_____

Your response

This is the longest of the four "Servant Songs" in Isaiah (42:1-9, 49:1-7, 50:4-9, and 52:13-53:12). It falls at the very center of 40:1-66:24 and is carefully

163

For Thought and Discussion: Having been "numbered with the transgressors," the Servant is able to make "intercession for the transgressors" (53:12). Why is this so? (Consider Hebrews 2:14-18, 4:15-16, 5:7-10.)

For Thought and Discussion: Can you identify with the way Isaiah describes us as straying sheep in 53:6? If so, how?

Optional Application: How are you prompted to respond to what Christ did for you?

Optional Application: Plan to meditate on a different phrase of 52:13-53:12 for ten minutes each day for the next week. For instance, think about the implications of "who has believed our message?" one day, and then "he carried our sorrows" the next. Let your meditation lead to confession, thanksgiving, praise.

composed of five stanzas with three verses each. All this shows the emphasis Isaiah strove to give this poem.

Although Jesus quoted Isaiah frequently, the Gospels never record that He quoted 52:13-53:12. He simply lived it. Even so, it is cited more often in the New Testament than any other Old Testament passage. The early Christians considered it the central explanation for Jesus' work on earth.

8. Have you experienced the peace and healing the Servant won for us by His punishment and wounds? If so, describe one way in which you have experienced this.

_____

_____

_____

_____

_____

9. Read through 52:13-53:12 again. Choose one phrase that seems especially significant to you, and meditate on it for awhile. Write what makes it important to you, and what implications it has for your life.

_____

_____

_____

_____

_____

_____

10. Is there any other response or application you would like to make? If so, write down your plans.

_____

_____

_____

_____

_____

11. List any questions you have about 52:13-53:12.

_____

_____

_____

_____

For the group

Warm-up. Let everyone sit and think silently about the griefs, sorrows, sicknesses, transgressions, and enmities they have seen and experienced during the past few days. After you read 52:13-53:12, consider for a moment how Jesus has borne all those griefs and sins.

Read aloud. Ask the reader to speak slowly and with meaning.

Summarize. What is the poem about?

Have someone remind the group of the purposes God declared in earlier chapters—liberating His people, proving to them and to the nations that He is the only God, proving His character, establishing peace and justice. Have someone else remind the group why Israel failed to be God's means of accomplishing His aims.

Questions. Questions 5 and 6 are most important for understanding what Christ has done for us. You might want to go carefully over each of the key phrases in 53:4-6,10-12 (*took up our infirmities, by his knowledge, justify many,* and so on).

Questions 8 through 10 allow you to become personal; ask people to decide specifically how they could respond this week to what Christ has done. You could pray together about this, and use some of the optional questions to prompt ideas.

Summarize.

Optional Application: a. Since Christians are called to be like Christ, in what ways is the "Suffering Servant" an example for us? (Can *we* carry other's sorrows [53:4]? Will we be "despised and rejected by men" if we follow Him?) You might see Luke 9:23-26; John 15:12-21; Romans 8:16-17; Galatians 4:19-20, 6:2; and Colossians 1:24-29.

b. How can you put these insights into practice by applying Luke 9:23 or Galatians 6:2? Talk with God about this.

c. However, see Psalm 49:7-8,15 and Galatians 6:5.

For Thought and Discussion: What does 52:13-53:12 reveal about God's nature?

For Thought and Discussion: How does 52:13-53:12 relate to God's purposes declared in 40:1-2,5,10-11; 42:6-9; 43:10-13; 44:6-7?

165

Wrap-up. In order to cover a lot of material, the next lesson asks you to choose two or three out of seven sets of passages. You can either have everyone do the same two or three, or have each person do different ones and report on what you've each learned. If you want everyone to cover all seven, plan two meetings to do so.

The lesson doesn't interpret the passages for you because Christians differ about them. If you want more background, look at one or two of the commentaries on pages 213-214, or choose another that you prefer.

Worship. Thank God for what He has done through the painful work of His Servant. Ask Him to guide and enable you to act as His servants in the world.

1. *Matthew Henry's Commentary*, volume 3.
2. *The NIV Study Bible*, page 1095; Young, volume 3, pages 343-345; compare KJV, NASB margin.
3. *The NIV Study Bible*, page 1018.
4. Young, volume 3, pages 338-339.
5. Young, volume 3, pages 348-349.
6. Young, volume 3, pages 357-358.

ISAIAH 40:1-66:24

The Kingdom of God

Peace, healing, acquittal—God promises these results of Jesus' work in 53:5,11. But if these are the beginnings of the restoration Christ bought for us, the Book of Comfort also depicts that restoration in many other ways. Like Jesus' parables of the Kingdom of God, each view of the Kingdom in Isaiah shows us one facet of the gem. This lesson will introduce you to a few of those facets and point you to others that you can study on your own later.

For Further Study: End-time prophecies are difficult. Read how scholars from several points of view interpret passages that confuse you. Consider some of the commentaries on page 213-214.

Study Skill—End-time Passages

When we study passages about the "end times," we need to keep in mind what Jesus taught about the Kingdom of God. On the one hand, He proclaimed that the Kingdom of God had begun because the King—Jesus Himself—had come. The end times began with Jesus' first coming. On the other hand, He promised to bring the Kingdom of God to its fulfillment when He came a second time.

For this reason, the prophecies in Isaiah about the restoration sometimes refer to what Jesus began at His first coming and will finish at His return. At other times, a prophecy refers only to what Jesus finished at His first coming or to what He will begin at His second. As we study one of these prophecies, we should ask ourselves both "To what extent does this describe what Jesus has already

(continued on page 168)

167

(continued from page 167)
done or is doing?" and "To what extent does this describe what will be true when Jesus returns?"

Another potential source of confusion is that many of Isaiah's prophecies also spoke to the immediate "end times" for which the exiles in Babylon were looking—the day when God would bring them home to the promised land. So, we should also ask, "To what extent does this describe something God did after the Babylonian exile?"

In this lesson are seven sets of passages. Choose two or three of the sets. Then study your selected passages and write down:

  a. what the passage(s) say about the restoration God promises to bring;
  b. how the passage(s) were fulfilled at Jesus' first coming;
  c. what the passage(s) might reveal about the time of Jesus' second coming;
  d. what the passage(s) teach you about the Kingdom of God;
  e. how the passages apply to our lives between the comings.

Remember that a given passage does not necessarily refer to the captives in Babylon *and* to Jesus' first coming *and* to His return. In such a case, leave some of the answer spaces blank.

Also, don't be concerned if you can't imagine just how Jesus will fulfill a prophecy at His return. The exact details of how God will usher in His Kingdom are unclear, but you can look for the impressions Isaiah evokes, a sense of God's plan, and an indication of how His Kingdom will differ from our present world. Humility can come from knowing that we don't have all the answers; the Lord tells us enough to motivate our response in the present.

Finally, you may not come up with a personal application for each of the "my response" spaces. One good application that you really intend to act upon is much better than answers for all the "my response" spaces and action on none of them.

If you finish two or three of the sets of passages and have time to do more, go ahead.

Sample answers are given for the first two sets of passages. Your answers may differ, but the examples should help you understand the questions.

A highway (40:3-5, 42:14-17, 43:16-21, 49:8-13)

In part, these passages predicted what was going to happen at the end of the Babylonian exile. The Lord led the Jews out of Babylon and back to Judah on a safe route.[1] He did not literally level the mountains. But the Jews who returned to Judah were those who had prepared spiritually to take the risky journey to the promised land. Many thousands of Jews remained in Babylon, content with their life there or fearful of change.

1. what the passages say about the restoration (observations)

   A highway will be built in the desert for a procession led by the Lord, Israel's King. In 40:3-5, someone is told to prepare a smooth path for the Lord's approach; in the other passages, He promises to build the highway Himself.

   how this was fulfilled at Jesus' first coming

   God sent John the Baptist to tell the Jews to prepare for the coming Messiah by repenting of their sins (Luke 3:4-6).

   what these passages might reveal about Jesus' second coming (interpretation)

   God will overcome all obstacles to Jesus' return. Jesus will safely and regally lead His people into His kingdom. People need to prepare spiritually to join that journey.

For Thought and Discussion: What kinds of people will be forbidden to travel on the highway with the Lord (35:8, 42:17)? Why will they be refused?

169

what I learn about God's Kingdom (interpretation)

On the one hand, God will clear the path to it. On the other hand, we must prepare ourselves in order that God may come to clear the path. The Kingdom requires God's initiative and power, as well as our active response.

how this applies to our lives between the comings (application)

We need to prepare for Jesus to come into our lives and lead us into His Kingdom. The Holy Spirit clears the highway in me and my life if I cooperate; He guides me daily on level paths toward God's Kingdom. Also, we need to prepare personally for Jesus' return, and we need to join in preparing the Church and in helping others to prepare.

my personal response

First, I give thanks that the Lord is leading me and others home from exile. Second, I need to practice consciously turning my thoughts to my destination: God's Kingdom. Third, I plan to set aside 10 minutes a day for the next week to let the Holy Spirit prepare a way for the Lord to come more fully into my life, and also to consider where His highway is taking me in the near future. My preparation should include confession and repentance (Matthew 3:1-3), as well as thanksgiving

Do you have another response? _____

**For Thought and
Discussion:** What
can any of the sets of
passages in this les-
son tell us about our-
selves and our
needs?

_____

_____

_____

Water in the desert (41:17-20, 43:19-21, 49:10, 51:3)

The route from Babylon to Judah went through dry
desert, but God provided literal water along the way
and in the promised land. He also provided spiritual
water—His presence—for the returnees. However,
Isaiah is probably using the return from Babylon
mostly as a symbol of a greater liberation.[2]
      If you prefer, just write answers for 41:17-20.

2. what the passages say about the restoration

> The Lord provides water in the desert
> so that the needy may drink and plants
> may flourish.

_____

how this was fulfilled at Jesus' first coming
(John 7:37-39)

_____

_____

_____

_____

what these passages may reveal about Jesus'
second coming

_____

_____

_____

_____

171

For Thought and Discussion: What does water represent in the Scriptures? (Use a concordance to find references.)

what I learn about the Kingdom

_____

_____

_____

_____

_____

how this applies to our lives between the comings

_____

_____

_____

_____

_____

my personal response _____

_____

_____

_____

_____

The Holy Spirit (44:1-5)

The outpouring of the Spirit was promised for the "descendants" (44:3) of the exiles; it would occur in the Messianic Age. Some relevant cross-references are Isaiah 11:2, 32:15; Jeremiah 31:33-34; Ezekiel 36:26-27; Joel 2:28-32.

3. what the passage says about the restoration

_____

_____

_____

how this was fulfilled at (or just after) Jesus'
first coming (*Optional:* See Mark 1:4-8, Acts
2:1-21.)

_____

_____

_____

_____

_____

what this passage may reveal about Jesus'
second coming

_____

_____

_____

_____

what I learn about the Kingdom _____

_____

_____

_____

_____

how this applies to our lives between the
comings

_____

_____

_____

_____

my personal response _____

_____

_____

Mother Zion (54:1-17)

Several of Isaiah's prophecies speak of Zion as the Lord's wife and the people's mother; you could look at 49:14-26, 50:1-3, or 62:1-12 for comparison to this passage. We chose 54:1-17 because it clearly follows from the Servant's triumphs in 52:13-53:12.

Jerusalem was repopulated after the exile, but the scale of 54:1-17 far exceeds the glory Jerusalem achieved in any century. The New Testament calls the Church and the heavenly Jerusalem Christ's bride and our mother.

Barren woman (54:1). Near Eastern people considered it a disgrace for a woman to be barren. When the Babylonians deported Jerusalem's population and broke the city's walls and buildings, she seemed like a woman bereft of husband and children.

Tent (54:2). Shepherd peoples lived in tents so that they could follow their flocks; a wife often had a tent separate from the men of the family. Here, Isaiah describes Jerusalem as a barren wife who has lived alone in her tent, but she will have to enlarge it to fit all her children.

Wife deserted (54:6). In 50:1, the Lord says that He never gave Zion a certificate of divorce, which was necessary to make a legal separation. Rather, He allowed a temporary separation when His "wife" rebelled against Him.

4. what the passage says about the restoration

174

how this was fulfilled at Jesus' first coming
(Acts 2:41, 4:4; Galatians 3:26-29, 4:21-31;
Ephesians 5:25-27; Hebrews 12:18-24)

_____

_____

_____

_____

_____

_____

what this passage may reveal about Jesus'
second coming (Revelation 21:1-4)

_____

_____

_____

_____

_____

what I learn about the Kingdom _____

_____

_____

_____

_____

_____

how this applies to our lives between the
comings

_____

_____

_____

_____

_____

my personal response _____

_____

_____

_____

_____

The nations come (60:1-22)

Here the Lord addresses Zion again. Be less concerned with the details (the place names, the particular gifts) than with the overall message of the
passage. Some people think it refers chiefly to what
will happen when Jesus returns as King, while
others think it refers mainly to the coming of the
Gentiles into the Church.[3]

Nothing like this occurred when the exiles
returned. Judah was repopulated, but the nation
remained poor and under the domination of one for-
eign empire after another.

The glory of the LORD (60:1). The Lord made His
presence known among the Israelites after the
exodus from Egypt in a burning cloud (Exodus
40:34-38). This cloud, which led the Israelites
through the desert and later abided between the
cherubim over the atonement cover in the Temple (Isaiah 37:16), was called "the glory of the
LORD." The glory (Hebrew: *shekinah*) was the
physical manifestation of God's invisible
presence.

Jesus displayed the glory when He lived
on earth (John 1:14). In a sense, He *was* the
glory—the physical manifestation of God's presence (Hebrews 1:3). Yet the glory was fully
apparent to human eyes only at the Transfigura-
tion (Luke 9:28-36).

5. what the passage says about the restoration

_____

_____

_____

_____

_____

_____

_____

how this was fulfilled at Jesus' first coming
(Matthew 2:1-12; John 1:4-5,9,14)

_____

_____

_____

_____

what this passage may reveal about Jesus'
return

_____

_____

_____

what I learn about the Kingdom _____

_____

_____

_____

_____

how this applies to our lives between the
comings

_____

For Further Study:
What is God's pur-
pose in telling us
about the Kingdom
(Romans 15:4,
1 Peter 1:10-13)?

_____

_____

_____

_____

my personal response _____

_____

_____

_____

_____

The year of the LORD (61:1-11)

In the Gospels, Jesus never used Isaiah 53 to describe His mission. Instead, He quoted Isaiah 61:1-2
(Luke 4:16-21). At that time, He did not mention
"the day of vengeance of our God" (61:2), which
would not occur until His second coming.

You might want to read all of chapter 61 but
focus on just the first few verses for your personal
meditation.

The year of the LORD's favor (61:2). The Law of
Moses stipulated a Year of Jubilee every fifty
years, when servants were set free, debts were
suspended, and land reverted to the families
who had originally owned it (Leviticus 25:10).
This law was almost never obeyed (Jeremiah
34:8-22), but it came to symbolize the time
when the Lord would liberate and restore all
things. (See also Isaiah 49:8, 63:4.)

Crown . . . ashes (61:3). On occasions of rejoicing,
people anointed their heads with oil and wore
elaborate headdresses. On occasions of mourning, people shaved their heads and covered
them with ashes.

178

6. what the passage says about the restoration

_____

_____

_____

_____

_____

how this was fulfilled at Jesus' first coming
(Mark 1:29-34, Acts 3:1-10)

_____

_____

_____

_____

what this may reveal about Jesus' second
coming

_____

_____

_____

_____

_____

what I learn about the Kingdom _____

_____

_____

_____

_____

_____

how this applies to our lives

_____

**For Thought and
Discussion:** a. What
kinds of people does
the Lord's Servant lib-
erate (61:1-3)?
   b. What does He
enable them to be
and do (61:4-7)?
   c. What do these
observations say
about who we are and
what we should do?
How could you act on
these conclusions?

**Optional
Application:**
a. Meditate on how
Jesus has fulfilled
61:1-3 for you.
   b. How could you
carry on Jesus' work
of 61:1-3?

For Thought and Discussion: Choose two of the prophecies in this lesson and use them to explain how God's Kingdom will be different from our world.

For Further Study: What do you learn from the metaphors about motherhood in 66:7-13? Verse 13 is one of the rare places where God likens Himself to a mother rather than a father, but notice that He comforts through Jerusalem. (See also Isaiah 49:13-15, 2 Corinthians 1:3-4.)

_____
_____
_____
_____

my personal response _____

_____
_____
_____
_____

New heavens, new earth (65:17-25, 66:7-24)

These passages speak of a "new earth" in terms familiar in this world. Nursing at Jerusalem's breast (66:11) is clearly figurative, but people interpret 65:20-25 and 66:17-24 in various ways. Some believe that these things will happen for a thousand years after Christ returns, and that afterward God will remake the heavens and the earth. Other people believe that these passages describe (literally or figuratively) what life will be like in the new earth.

For now, write down what you observe that these passages say about the future and what you learn from these passages about the Kingdom of God.

7. what the passages say _____

_____
_____
_____
_____
_____
_____
_____

what I learn about the Kingdom _____

_____

_____

_____

_____

For Further Study: Compare the prophecies in this lesson to 1 Thessalonians 4:13-5:11, Revelation 19:1-22:21.

how I should respond in the present to this future hope

_____

_____

_____

_____

_____

Your response

8. What are the most important insights you have had about the Kingdom of God from the passages in this lesson?

_____

_____

_____

_____

_____

_____

9. If you like, write down what difference you would like these insights to make to your present life. (You may have done this sufficiently in previous questions.)

_____

_____

_____

_____

_____

_____

10. List any questions you have about these
     passages.

_____

_____

_____

_____

For the group

Warm-up. What aspect of your world would each of
your group members most like to see change?

Choose passages. You will need to handle this lesson a bit differently because of the number of passages it contains. Consider one of the following
options:

   1. *If you have all studied the same passages.*
Briefly discuss the study skill and instructions on
pages 167-168. Make sure everyone understands
how a prophecy can apply to the time of Jesus' first
coming, the Church Age now, and the time of His
return. Then select as a group two sets of passages
to discuss. For each set of passages:
   Read part or all of the passages aloud.
   Summarize what the passages say about the
      restoration.
   Let any members who prepared this question
      tell how the passages apply to Jesus' first
      coming.
   Let the group discuss a) what the passages
      reveal about the Kingdom—what it is like
      and how it differs from our world; b) how
      the passages may be fulfilled at Jesus'
      return; c) how they apply to your lives;
      d) how you might respond.

182

2. *If you have studied different passages.* After discussing the Study Skill and instructions, plan to cover all seven sets of passages. You will have less time for depth on each one unless you take two meetings. To begin, read part of the first set of passages. Let someone summarize what the set of passages says, how it was fulfilled at Jesus' first coming, and how it may be fulfilled at His return. Then discuss what you learn about the Kingdom from this set of passages. Repeat this process for all seven sets of passages. Finally, discuss what impressions of the Kingdom you get from all of these passages and how you might respond.

Whichever approach you choose, stress that impressions of the Kingdom and present responses are more valuable than precise knowledge of details of the future. Expect your interpretations of the passages to vary. Try to discern which are reasonable views and which are not. Discuss why you favor one interpretation over another. If you like, have someone investigate what commentators say about a passage and report to the group.

Summarize. Sum up your impressions of the Kingdom and your plans for response.

Wrap-up.

Worship. Thank God for the hints He has given about the glories of His Kingdom. Thank Him for details of it that strike you. Pray, "your kingdom come," and ask God to enable you to respond today as He wills.

Kingdom Promises

God's covenant promises were tailored to His people. They were farmers, vine-growers, and herdsmen concerned with the fertility of land, livestock, and women. They feared disease, drought, barrenness, and hunger. But because Israel lay always between militaristic kingdoms of the Nile and the Euphrates, God's people lived ever in fear of invasion as well. Finally, the nation suffered ceaselessly from poor leadership, especially from rulers and judges indifferent to

(continued on page 184)

(continued from page 183)

the rights of the powerless. Therefore, when God described His Kingdom's blessings in terms of food, water, health, abundance, political stability, peace, and justice, He was speaking to the people's deepest longings.

Food and protection from invasion may be small concerns for affluent people in a stable nation. For them, other biblical promises of love, forgiveness, belonging, security, triumph, health, and endless life have more appeal. But behind all of the Bible's pictures of the Kingdom is the promise that our deepest needs will be met, both those we feel strongly and those we cannot name.

1. According to Leupold, volume 2, page 23, God had deserted His Temple before the exile because of the people's wickedness, but He returned after the exile and commanded the people to rebuild His Temple (Ezekiel 11:23, 43:1-5; Haggai 1:1-8). Thus God Himself was traveling on this highway back to Jerusalem.
2. The people who returned were able to grow crops in the promised land, but the arid parts of the land remained wilderness. Between 100 and 1950 AD, Palestine's deserts actually worsened. Young, volume 3, pages 91-92 says that Isaiah did not have the exiles primarily in mind. He thinks the water symbolizes all the needs God meets for the afflicted who look to Him.
3. *The NIV Study Bible*, page 1104.

ISAIAH 55:1-58:14

And So, an Invitation

Perhaps the new heavens and earth is the fitting place to end a study of Isaiah; after all, that is where the book ends. But the study would not be complete without a look at God's invitation to join in those joys. God welcomes into His Kingdom all who respond rightly to His invitation. The three passages in this lesson examine God's invitation and the response He desires.

The Seller (55:1-13)

Near Eastern cities were full of vendors striding through the crowds and calling out to draw attention to their wares. In dry times, even water had to be bought. Like a vendor in the marketplace, the Lord shouts "Ho!" (KJV), "Come!" (NIV). Read this chapter, noting what wares He offers and to whom He offers them.

1. The Lord cries out to "all you who are thirsty" and to "you who have no money" (55:1). Whom does He mean?

_____

_____

_____

_____

For Further Study:
a. What food and drink does Jesus offer in John 6:35,51,53-58?

b. What does He offer in John 7:37-39, 4:13-14?

c. How can you avail yourself of these offers?

185

2. He invites them to "come to the waters," to "buy wine and milk" (symbols of what is pleasant and nourishing) and to dine on "the richest of fare" (55:1-2). What is He offering?

_____

_____

_____

_____

3. Why does He invite the people to buy good things "without money and without cost" (55:1)? What point is He making?

_____

_____

_____

_____

_____

4. "Listen, listen," He implores (55:2), giving reasons why the thirsty and impoverished should listen, come, buy, and eat. How do modern people spend their money and labor on "what is not bread" and "what does not satisfy"?

_____

_____

_____

_____

_____

_____

Everlasting covenant (55:3). The Lord had promised David that one of his descendants would always be king of God's people; the last and permanent King would be the Messiah (2 Samuel 7:14-16, Isaiah 9:7). The titles "witness," "leader," and "commander" link the Servant's mission of

186

chapters 40-66 with the Son of David's position in chapters 9 and 11. The life and the covenant promised in 55:3-4 are the fare promised in 55:1-2.

5. In 55:6-9, God addresses the poor and thirsty from another perspective. He calls them "wicked" and "evil." Who are the thirsty, poor, wicked, evil ones in your day whom the Lord is calling?

_____

_____

_____

_____

_____

6. These people need to "seek" and "call on" the Lord "while he may be found" and "is near" (55:6). Why is there a time limit?

_____

_____

_____

_____

7. The Lord invites the poor to buy without cost, but 55:7-9 describes a cost: repentance. Why is it necessary to forsake one's wicked "way" and "thoughts" before one can turn to the Lord and be pardoned (55:7-9)?

_____

_____

_____

_____

_____

Optional Application: a. Does 55:1,7 apply to you? To whom else does it apply?

b. How could you show the same attitude toward the thirsty and wicked that God shows in 55:1-9?

For Thought and Discussion: What does it mean to "seek" and "call on" the Lord? How do you do these things?

For Thought and Discussion:
a. Why is pardon free (55:1,7) even though one must forsake and turn (55:7)?

b. What did our salvation cost Jesus, and why did it cost Him that (53:5-9)?

c. Do we have to "do" or "give" anything to obtain this gift? If so, how is what we give different from work to earn salvation?

d. On the topic of salvation's cost, see questions 3, 7, 11, 12, and 17.

Optional Application: Make a list of some areas in which your ways and thoughts are different from God's. For example, do you freely pardon those who sin against you (55:7)? For some other ideas, see Luke 6:35-36. Also, consider what you have observed about God in earlier parts of Isaiah.

Optional Application: Reflect on the implications of 55:1-2 or 55:6-7 for your life. How could you seek, call on, come to, drink from, and eat from the Lord more fully this week? Why should you do these things?

For Thought and Discussion: What impression of the Lord's character do you get from 55:1-13?

For Further Study: The fulfillment of Isaiah 56:1-8 came as a great shock to the Jews. See Acts 8:26-39, 10:1-11:18.

8. God promises liberation, joy, peace, and abundance for those who seek Him while He may be found (55:12-13). How do we know that God's promises are trustworthy (55:10-11)?

_____

_____

_____

_____

_____

9. How does 55:1-13 make you want to respond?

_____

_____

_____

_____

_____

Eunuchs and foreigners (56:1-8)

In chapter 55, the Lord not only welcomed but begged the destitute and the wicked to come to Him humbly. In 56:1-8, He opens the gates of the Kingdom still wider.

Sabbath (56:2,4,6). Refraining from work on the Sabbath day was not the highest commandment, but it was an outward sign of love for God and commitment to the covenant.[1] Isaiah 58:13 points out the essence of Sabbath-keeping: neither "going your own way" nor "doing as you please" nor "speaking idle words" when you are resting from work; and considering the rest day "a delight."

Foreigner (56:3,6). Members of certain nations were forbidden by the Law to join God's people until the third or even tenth generation had lived in

188

Israel (Deuteronomy 23:3,7-8). By this law, God stressed His abhorrence of the practices of those nations.

Eunuch (56:3,4). The Law also forbade men who had been emasculated from joining God's people, even if they were Israelites by birth (Deuteronomy 23:1). Pagan nations often emasculated boys on purpose to make loyal civil servants, but God wanted to keep Israel from doing this. His holiness could be approached only by physically and morally perfect people—a rule applied especially strictly to the priests (Leviticus 21:16-23). Isaiah 56:3-6 was a radically new welcome to flawed people.

10. Why does the Servant's work make birth, heritage, past history, and physical flaws no longer barriers to approaching the Holy God (56:1-8)? (*Optional:* See Isaiah 53:4-5; Colossians 1:21-23, 2:13-15.)

_____

_____

_____

_____

_____

11. In 56:1, does the Lord say that righteous behavior will *earn* salvation or that it is the right *response to* the coming salvation? How can you tell?

_____

_____

_____

_____

_____

12. What present response does God expect from those whom He invites into His Kingdom of salvation (56:1-2,4,6)?

For Thought and Discussion: Eunuchs and foreigners represented defiled people in ancient Israel, like prostitutes and tax collectors in Jesus' time. Who are the defiled and scorned people in your day?

Optional Application: Is it important to you that people with flawed bodies or unbelieving parents are now welcome into God's Kingdom? If so, how do you think you should respond?

Optional Application: In 56:1-8 the Lord stresses keeping the Sabbath. How does this apply to you as a Christian? (You might consider Luke 6:1-11, 13:10-17, 14:1-6; Hebrews 4:1-11, 10:23-25.)

For Thought and Discussion: In 55:7 and 56:2, repentance is described as forsaking evil. How is it possible for us to forsake evil?

Optional Application: How can you seek to do what pleases the Lord rather than yourself on His holy day, and at the same time consider this submission a delight?

For Thought and Discussion: a. What difference does it make to you that God dwells in the lofty place that befits His rank and also with those who are crushed and humble?

b. What does this fact show about His character?

c. What does it mean to be contrite and humble?

d. How can you become more like this?

The Lofty One (57:14-21)

After condemning Judah's idolatry (57:1-13), the Lord returns to the theme of building a highway for the return of His true people. He rejects from His Kingdom those who persist in wickedness (57:13,20-21), for the true Israel is a holy people who can dwell with a Holy God.

13. Isaiah names three characteristics of God in 57:15a. What is true of God?

_____

_____

_____

14. God says He dwells in a high and holy place and *also* with the contrite (penitent, crushed) and lowly (57:15b). The high and holy place is reasonable for the High and Lofty One (57:15a). However, why does God dwell with the lowly and contrite? (*Optional:* See Deuteronomy 10:17-19, Matthew 11:29, 1 Peter 5:5-6, 1 John 1:5-10.)

_____

_____

_____

_____

15. Specifically how could the aspects of God's character in 57:15 affect your attitudes and actions this week?

_____

_____

_____

_____

_____

Optional Application: Ask the Lord what you could do in response to His mercy, along the lines of 58:6-14. You may need to be persistent in this prayer over some time, to show the Lord that you are serious.

True fasting (58:6-14)

In lesson thirteen you looked at chapter 58 as an account of Israel's failure to be God's servant. But in a positive way, the passage also describes the joys of the Kingdom made available to persons of a certain character.

16. What Kingdom benefits does the Lord offer in 58:6-14?

_____

_____

_____

_____

_____

_____

17. The activities in 58:6-14 are not works by which a person earns salvation, but rather deeds that flow from the character of the repentant one whom God has saved. What kinds of things does the pardoned person do?

_____

_____

_____

_____

_____

_____

Optional Application: Plan time today to worship God for His character. Then ask Him to show you how you could live more in accord with His nature. As you pray, you might meditate on 55:1-2, 6-7 or 57:15.

Your response

18. Is there one insight from the passages in this lesson that you would like to apply to yourself this week? If so, write it down, along with any ideas you have about how you might apply it.

_____

_____

_____

_____

_____

19. List any questions you have about this lesson.

_____

_____

_____

_____

For the group.

Warm-up. Ask the group to think silently about this question: "Is there anything for which you are really *hungry* or *thirsty*? If so, what is that thing?" Let people answer aloud if they wish.

Read aloud. You can read the four passages all at once or as you come to them.

Summarize. Quickly summarize what each of the four passages is about.

The Seller. Each passage in this lesson focuses on these three themes:

> What does God offer?
> What responses does He expect?
> What character traits does He show?

You might want to concentrate on just one theme. For example, the cost of salvation is addressed in

192

questions 3, 7, 11, 12, 17, and a "For Thought and Discussion." Be sure to stress the difference between responding to grace and working to earn salvation. It runs counter to firmly rooted notions most of us grow up with.

Many people find it easier to identify with being spiritually thirsty or materially lacking than with being wicked (55:7). Help the group to identify with both (compare Luke 5:32) and to grapple with the high demands God places on us—utter repentance from evil acts and thoughts. Several questions deal with repentance.

Eunuchs and foreigners. Again, the point is God's open, free invitation to anyone who will respond, even those despised in Jewish culture. Also, the response God expects is drastic (56:2).

Opinions vary as to whether Christians are bound to keep a Sabbath and if so, how. If necessary, refer people to authorities they respect and to Genesis 2:1-3; Exodus 20:8-11; Matthew 5:17-20, 12:1-14. Many books also deal with the Sabbath. You probably won't have time to discuss this question now, but you could plan another meeting and agree to study relevant scriptures and various alternate opinions.

The Lofty One.

True fasting. As before, the focus is God's offer, His character, and our response. You could spend more time analyzing the sins and devising ways of personally acting on what God urges. You might even plan a whole meeting to explore how you could act on this chapter in your families and community.

Wrap-up. The final lesson in this study is a review of the whole book. Its purpose is to help you pull together the book's themes into a consistent whole. This will help you see and remember connections. You could easily spend hours doing a thorough review, so urge group members not to feel pressed to do more than they can.

The review will also give you a chance to assess the results of your efforts to apply Isaiah to your lives. This should let you reconsider how you are going about application; it should not just make you feel guilty. Remind the group before they review that application is not done to measure up to

193

anyone's expectations of what a good Christian is.
Remind them of 55:1,7 and 57:15.

Worship. Praise God for His character. Thank Him
for what He offers us. Ask Him for the grace to truly
forsake evil and respond to Him wholeheartedly. Let
yourselves be contrite and humble.

1. Kidner, page 620; *The NIV Study Bible*, page 1099; Young,
volume 3, pages 389-390.

LESSON EIGHTEEN

REVIEW

Looking Back

It's easy to lose track of the overall message of a book by the time you have studied individual passages for sixteen weeks. So, in this final lesson we will try to pull together some of the themes we have been tracing. Most of the questions below cite many verses from the whole book, but you should feel free to look up only as many references as you like, or even simply to page through the book looking for passages that prompt your memory. The verses offered in the questions are intended only as aids to your memory.

1. According to 1:2-4, for what crime was Isaiah sent to indict Israel?

_____

2. One theme of Isaiah's message is "the LORD is salvation."

What sources of salvation competed for Judah's loyalty?

1:10-17 _____

2:6-8 _____

3:1-3 _____

3:18-23 _____

5:8 _____

For Further Study:
a. Read the book of Isaiah straight through. This is the best way to begin reviewing a book of the Bible.
    b. Make your own outline of the book. You can use some of the many outlines in commentaries and study Bibles as models.

For Thought and Discussion: What does "salvation" mean?

195

5:11 _____

8:12-13 _____

20:1-6 _____

24:1-2 _____

28:14-15 _____

31:1 _____

36:8 _____

44:12-20 _____

57:1-10 _____

3. How did the Lord demonstrate that all other
   sources of salvation were hopeless? (Recall
   some of the ways in 3:1; 5:9; 7:14,17; 8:6-8;
   9:6-7,13-15; 10:12; 11:1-16; 24:21-22; 37:6-7,
   36-38; 38:1-8; 40:12-31; 41:1-4,17-20,25-29;
   44:24-45:7; 47:1; 52:13-53:12.)

_____

_____

_____

_____

_____

_____

_____

_____

_____

_____

_____

4. Did the Lord declare Himself to be salvation
   only for the people of Judah (49:6, 55:1,
   56:1-8)? Explain.

196

_____

_____

_____

_____

5. According to Isaiah's book, what does the Lord do when we lean on something other than Him for security or salvation?

_____

_____

_____

_____

6. How does Isaiah portray Christ and His mission (7:14, 9:1-7, 11:1-16, 42:1-7, 49:1-7, 50:4-9, 52:13-53:12)?

_____

_____

_____

_____

_____

_____

7. What have you learned from Isaiah about the Kingdom of God (2:1-5, 4:2-6, 9:1-7, 11:1-16, 25:6-8, 35:1-10, 40:3-5, 41:17-20, 44:1-5, 54:1-10, 60:1-22, 61:1-11, 65:17-25, 66:7-24)?

_____

_____

_____

_____

_____

Optional Application: What needs or longings do you feel most strongly? How would you most like to experience God's salvation in your present situation? Pray about this, and ask God to save you.

Optional Application: What implications do questions 2, 3, and 5 have for you?

For Thought and Discussion: What does Isaiah reveal about God's plan for mankind? About the Jews' place in that plan? About Christ's place?

For Thought and Discussion: a. How does Isaiah reflect these aspects of the Lord's character: mercy, justice, faithfulness, sovereignty?

b. How does God show grace in this book (1:9,18-20; 53:1-12; 55:7)?

_____

_____

_____

_____

_____

8. Write down three of the most memorable insights you have gained from Isaiah about God's character or plan.

_____

_____

_____

_____

_____

_____

_____

_____

9. How would you summarize Isaiah's message to God's people?

_____

_____

_____

_____

_____

Study Skill—Application

Whenever you take stock of how you are applying Scripture, remember:

1. Change is slow. It may take years for a new attitude to take root.

2. Change is hidden. You may be the last person to notice real changes in yourself, and

(continued on page 199)

(continued from page 198)
the first to imagine changes that you only wish have occurred.

3. Change is by the Holy Spirit. Tearful repentance, confession, steady obedience, and painful resistance of temptation are all part of the Christian life; self-condemnation, anxiety, and will-power are not. Self-reliance is spiritual pride.

10. Have you noticed any areas (thoughts, attitudes, opinions, behavior) in which you have changed as a result of studying Isaiah? If so, how have you changed?

_____

_____

_____

_____

_____

_____

11. a. Look back over the entire study at questions in which you expressed a desire to make some specific application. Are you satisfied with your follow-through?

Pray about any areas that you would like to continue to pursue or begin to concentrate on. What lessons from Isaiah would you like to apply more to your daily life?

_____

_____

_____

_____

_____

_____

b. If you have any plans for specific action to

take these lessons to heart during the coming
weeks, you can write those plans below.

_____

_____

_____

_____

_____

_____

12. Review the questions you listed at the end of
    lessons one through seventeen. Do any of your
    questions remain unanswered? If so, you could
    check one of the sources listed on pages
    213-216, bring up your questions again in your
    group, or ask someone knowledgeable. Consider
    looking for cross-references on your own.

For the group

Warm-up. Ask group members how they have experienced the Lord being salvation during the past
week.

Review of the book. We normally begin a review by
reading the book straight through. However, since
Isaiah is too long for most people to read at once,
we have simply urged students to leaf back and
forth through the book to remind themselves of
Isaiah's words.

　　We have structured this review around one of
Isaiah's themes—"the LORD is salvation"—because
it suggests so many aspects of the Lord's character
and so many meanings of the word *salvation*. Isaiah
shows the people seeking deliverance from all kinds
of ills (physical, political, economic, spiritual) and
he shows the Lord healing each of those ills. So,
explore the different kinds of needs people try to
meet, the various means of salvation they try, and
the ways the Lord meets each need and frustrates
each false attempt. You could take time then to discuss your needs and how you try to meet them.

　　Your goal in each question is to look at some
specific passages about salvation or Christ or what-

ever and then to summarize Isaiah's teaching about this in a few sentences. Try to express a few important impressions of Isaiah's message coherently enough for everyone to remember. Aim for clear statements that give the group something they can recall a year from now when they want to study Isaiah again or tell someone what they know about Isaiah.

Try to get the group to summarize the book in some other way than just "the LORD is salvation."

Review of application. To keep the group from trying to save face by making up inner transformations that have not been so dramatic, draw attention to the Study Skill on pages 198-199. Then give everyone a chance to share what he or she has been trying to apply.

One kind of application has to do with attitudes. Someone might say, "I've been praying to grow more trusting in the midst of my circumstances, but I still feel anxious. I know why I don't need to feel anxious, but I do anyway. It's frustrating." The group may need to pray consistently for this person. He can plan to meditate on scriptures about trust and to keep praying faithfully. Constant prayer is about all we can do about attitudes like trust until we encounter a decision that lets us act in either trust or fear. At that moment, the tree rooted in prayer and God's Word should bear fruit. If not, a believer must *know* that confession and repentance will bring forgiveness and a chance to try again. Encourage this person to keep praying and to look for moments of decision like these.

Another kind of application deals with actions. Isaiah 58 calls for active hospitality, generosity, and involvement in others' lives. Someone might say, "I know I'm not serving other people in these basic ways; I'm too involved in doing what I want. But I can't figure out whom to feed or clothe or house or aid." The group could talk about the needs of people in that person's church, family, or community. You could plan to act together. You could point out what this person does for others and consider what occupies his time. He may be taking on a false burden or a true one. He may be trying to do more than his body can handle or facing up to a real desire of God.

All of these possibilities can lead to a rich discussion. Try to let group members advise and encourage rather than letting them expect answers from the leader. In general, it is best never to do something for the group that it can do for itself.

Questions. Be sure to let group members raise their unanswered questions. Again, don't answer anything that the group could answer. You can direct members to books or cross-references if necessary.

Evaluation. Take a few minutes or all of your next meeting to evaluate how your group functioned during your study of Isaiah. Some questions you might ask are:

> How well did the study help you to grasp the book of Isaiah?
> What did you like best about your meetings?
> What did you like least? What would you change?
> How well did you meet the goals you set at your first meeting?
> What did you learn about small group study?
> What are members' current needs and interests?
> What will you do next?

Worship. Thank God for all the ways in which He is your salvation. Thank Him for what He has taught you about Himself through the book of Isaiah. Ask Him to enable you to live in light of what you have learned.

ISAIAH 13:1-23:18

Oracles Against the Nations

Isaiah's primary mission was to Judah, but he had an international portfolio as well. God sent warnings to some pagan nations so that they, like Israel, would be without excuse when judgment fell. Isaiah also prophesied against nations with whom Judah was considering alliances; those words were meant to warn Judah to rely on no one but the Lord.

You may want to look at just a few of the oracles in this section. Look for the kinds of matters that concern the Lord and the ways He deals with nations. We've tried to give you enough historical background to understand the contexts of each prophecy. Some of the places mentioned are on the map on page 9.

Many of the questions in this lesson ask you what the passage tells you about God. This is nearly always a good question to ask yourself when you are studying a passage of Scripture. Another good one is "What does this passage tell about people in general and me in specific?"

Babylon (13:1-14:23)

This prophecy applies to Babylon as the most important city of the Assyrian Empire,[1] as the capital of the Babylonian Empire of the next century,[2] and as the symbol of all world empires opposed to the Lord (13:9-13). The New Testament uses Babylon as a symbol in this way (1 Peter 5:13; Revelation 14:8, 16:19, 17:1-18:24).

This oracle is remarkable for its details, fulfilled at various times over centuries. The Medes (13:17) allied with the Babylonians in overthrowing Assyria in 612-609 BC. They then followed Cyrus to defeat Babylon in 539. The city of Babylon was renowned for its beauty (13:19); "the hanging gardens of Nebuchadnezzar were one of the seven wonders of the ancient world."[3] But the city declined after Cyrus conquered it, and in the fourth century BC a new emperor built his capital forty miles away.[4] By 600 AD, Babylon was utterly deserted.[5]

1. Why does the Lord cry out against pride and arrogance so often (13:9-13, 14:12-21)?

2. How is 13:19-22 a warning for modern nations?

3. What is the fate of one who tries to gain power by oppressing others (14:3-11)? See especially verses 10-11.

4. What happens to one who aspires to have the most beauty and the highest status (14:12-21)? See especially verses 15,19.

5. In 14:4-21, "the king of Babylon" is symbolic of all kings and others who aspire to take God's place. Some people have seen this as a picture of Satan's fall from grace.
   How can a person really become "like the Most High" (14:14)? Contrast Philippians 2:5-11 with Isaiah 14:13-15.

6. Isaiah 14:1-2 contains the seed of chapters 40-66. How will Israel's restoration to authority be possible (14:1)?

7. What does 13:1-14:23 tell you about God's character and interests?

Assyria (14:24-27)

8. The words *plan, intention,* and *purpose* recur in 14:24-27. What point is the Lord making by repeating these words?

9. What do you notice about the Lord in 14:24-27?

Philistia (14:28-32)

In 715 BC, revolts in the north were preoccupying King Sargon of Assyria, and Philistia took the opportunity to revolt. The Philistines sent an embassy to Hezekiah in Jerusalem to urge him to join their rebellion. The patriotic Hezekiah was eager to do so, but Isaiah gave him the counsel of 14:28-32.

10. According to 14:29-30, was there any human hope of ousting Assyria? Why?

11. To what hope did Isaiah want Hezekiah to cling in the face of temptation to make alliances with men (14:32)?

Moab (15:1-16:14)

Sargon's army ravaged Moab in 715-713 BC. This oracle depicts the flight of refugees after Moab's strongholds have been taken.

12. The Lord judged Moab's pride (16:6) by destruction. Still, how did He feel about the suffering people (15:5; 16:9,11)?

13. The Lord counseled the striken Moabites to send tribute to Jerusalem as a sign of humbling themselves as subjects (16:1). How can Jerusalem be a hope for Moab (16:3-5)?

14. Consider how Jerusalem is supposed to treat the refugees (16:1-5). Are there any implications here for the way the Church treats unbelievers who seek mercy? If so, what are they?

Damascus (17:1-14)

This oracle dates from between 740 and 732 BC, when Damascus and Israel were allies and not yet destroyed. That is why the Lord interweaves words against Israel with words against Damascus.

15. Most Israelites will die as rebels and worshipers of what "their fingers have made," but a few gleanings will survive this harvest of judgment

(17:4-8). What will those who abandon their own creations trust instead (17:7-8)?

16. When God's people try to produce good things while ignoring the Lord, what happens (17:10-11)?

Cush (18:1-7)

This is a region now called Sudan and Ethiopia, an area thick with "whirring" insects. The Cushites sent envoys to Hezekiah (18:2), urging him to ally for defense. Isaiah tells in this prophecy how the Lord deals with threats to His people when they trust in Him.

17. What does 18:3-7 tell you about God's methods, character, and abilities?

Egypt (19:1-25)

18. In 19:1-15, the Lord speaks to Egypt as a worldly power, one on which Judah was often tempted to rely (20:5). Egypt was known for its fertility and for the skill and learning of its leaders.

    What does 19:1-15 show about worldly wisdom and organization?

19. Verses 16-25 list four announcements of Egypts's future. They look beyond the near future of Isaiah's time to God's acts in the last days.

    List the four sets of events Isaiah foresees in 19:16-17, 19:18, 19:19-22, and 19:23-25.

20. Consider the spiritual state of Egypt in Isaiah's day as portrayed in 19:1-15. What does 19:16-25 tell you about God's power and ultimate aims?

Cush and Egypt (20:1-6)

An Assyrian monument erected in Ashdod explains this prophecy. In 713 BC, the Philistine city Ashdod revolted against Assyria (recall 14:28-32). Assyria deposed Ashdod's king, but a new leader named

Yamani continued the struggle. Cush and Egypt promised to help, and Ashdod also appealed to Judah. At that point, Isaiah began to wear the clothes of a slave—loincloth and bare feet—without explanation. His silent warning apparently convinced King Hezekiah, for Judah did not help Ashdod and so was not squashed along with that city. In 711, Sargon finally defeated Ashdod. Yamani fled to Cush, whose ruler promptly gave him up to Assyria. Egypt, too, broke its promise to fight.

21. Consider the potential results of disobeying God in this crisis. Is there a lesson here for Christians?

22. Think about Isaiah's method of communicating God's message (20:2). What do you think is the purpose of this approach?

Babylon (21:1-10)

Isaiah foresaw Babylon's fall to the Elamites and Medes in 539 BC one hundred years before Babylon even became the dominant power in the region.

23. What does this prophecy show about the Lord's control over history?

24. Think about Isaiah's reaction to this vision of the deaths of Israel's persecutors (21:3-4). Does this reaction tell you anything about Isaiah himself?

Edom (21:11-12)

Here, Isaiah sees someone calling to a watchman on the walls of Seir, the capital of Edom. The someone wants to know the time of night—that is, how much longer will the night of oppression under Assyria go on? The watchman replies that Assyria's night will end soon, but the morning of peace will be brief before Babylon brings a new night.

The Hebrew for the verse "ask . . . ask . . . come back yet again" (21:12) could also be translated, "seek . . . turn (or repent) . . . come."[6]

25. Why would Isaiah say to a pagan nation, "If you would seek, then turn and come"?

207

Arabia (21:13-17)

The Dedanites were an Arabian merchant tribe. Their caravans had to hide in thickets when Assyria and later Babylon attacked Arabia.[7]

Jerusalem (22:1-25)

Now the Lord shows Isaiah Jerusalem under siege, either in 701 BC when Assyria tried and failed, or in 587/586 when Babylon tried and succeeded. "The Valley of Vision" (22:1) is either Jerusalem (a hill surrounded by mountains) or a valley somewhere in or around Jerusalem where Isaiah saw most of his visions.[8]

26. Observe the people's various responses to imminent death in 22:1,3,8-11,13. (Note: Pagans often offered incense to the gods on rooftops.)

27. How did Isaiah respond, and how did the Lord want all of Jerusalem to respond (22:4,11-12)?

Shebna (22:15) was "master of the palace," the office second only to the king (Isaiah 22:21, 1 Kings 4:6, 2 Kings 15:5).[9] He reacted to death by scheming to obtain a tomb cut from rock, such as a king would have, so that later generations would assume he was important (22:15-16).

28. The Lord was furious at Shebna's plans (22:17-19); He called the high official "this steward" (22:15). Why was He angry?

29. The Lord describes the bestowal of authority on Eliakim in appropriate Hebrew terms (22:20-24). What light does 22:22 shed on Matthew 16:17-19 and Revelation 3:7? (Remember that Eliakim was being made the king's right hand man, not king himself.)

Eliakim and Shebna appear in Isaiah 36:1-3 as officials under Hezekiah. Eliakim is master of the palace and Shebna is merely a secretary. Apparently, the events of chapter 36 occurred shortly after the demotion described in chapter 22.

The point of 22:23-25 is that Eliakim will be a source of strength for Judah and an honor to his family for a while, but even he will eventually give way under the pressures of the times.

30. What does 22:1-25 reveal about God?

Tyre (23:1-18)

Tyre was the main seaport on the Phoenician coast, "the marketplace of the nations" (23:3). Part of the city was a fortress built on two rocky islands offshore. Tyrian traders traveled as far as the English Channel and the Indian Ocean. Tyre was known as a cosmopolitan, immoral city dedicated to the desires of merchants and sailors. Sidon (23:2,4,12) was Phoenicia's second major city, north of Tyre. Ships of Tarshish (23:1) were Tyre's large trading vessels. This oracle is portrayed as news of Tyre's destruction brought to Cyprus, Tyre's nearest colony.[10]

31. Describe what you observe about Tyre's values and morals from 23:6-9,12,16-17.

32. What might the Lord mean by calling Tyre a "prostitute" city (23:15-17)?

33. Compare Isaiah 23:15-17 to Revelation 17:1-5, 18:1-3. Compare Isaiah 23:18 to Revelation 21:24.

34. What lessons does this prophecy offer us today about materialism?

Summary

35. Summarize what you have learned from 13:1-23:18 about . . .

the Lord's character, values, plans, and methods;

human nature and needs;

Isaiah's overall message to Judah.

36. Does anything in these chapters suggest a personal application for you? If so, write down what seems relevant and what you plan to do about it.

For Thought and Discussion: How does all this woe and discussion against the *nations* fit into Isaiah's message for *Judah*?

For Thought and Discussion: a. How does 13:1-23:18 suggest that God regards modern nations? Why do you think so?
    b. Why is this important for Christians to know? How should God's view of the nations affect what we do and think?

209

For the group

Warm-up. Ask, "What one aspect of the current world situation would you like God to do something about?"

Read aloud. It probably won't be practical to read all of 13:1-23:18 aloud. Instead, choose just one section to read, such as 13:9-13.

Summarize. Summarize the main ideas Isaiah is trying to get across in 13:1-23:18. What is the main message that runs through all of these scattered prophecies?

Questions. Choose just one or two of the prophecies to discuss in detail. Save time to discuss the summary questions and the "For Thought and Discussion" questions on page 209.

Worship. Praise God for His sovereign control over the nations. Thank Him that you can count on His justice and protection.

1. *The NIV Study Bible,* page 1035.
2. Young, volume 1, pages 409-415; Kidner, page 599.
3. *The NIV Study Bible,* page 1036.
4. Kidner, page 599.
5. *The NIV Study Bible,* page 1036.
6. Kidner, page 602.
7. *The NIV Study Bible,* page 1046.
8. Young, volume 2, pages 85-86; Kidner, page 602; Leupold, volume 1, page 345.
9. Roland de Vaux, *Ancient Israel: Volume 1: Social Institutions* (New York: McGraw-Hill Book Company, 1966), pages 129-131; Young, volume 2, page 114.
10. *The NIV Study Bible,* page 1048; Kidner, page 603.

GOING ON IN ISAIAH

Ideas for Further Study

Obviously, we have only scratched the surface of Isaiah's book in this study. If you would like to look into it some more on your own, you could just go back through it passage by passage, drawing out the meaning of each passage as a whole and of each verse in it. You could read through, looking for verses to memorize and meditate on in context. Or, you could try one of the suggestions below.

1. Look for all the names and titles for God (see page 32-33), and consider prayerfully what they tell you about Him.

2. Compare the prophecies of taking leaders away (such as 3:1-3, 9:13-17, 19:15) to the role of the Messiah (9:1-7, 11:1-16, etc.)

3. Meditate on the foolishness of idols (40:18-31, 41:21-29, 44:6-23, 45:18-25, 46:1-13).

4. Using a concordance, find and study all of Isaiah's references to one of the following:
    righteousness
    justice
    peace
    salvation/Savior
    redemption/Redeemer

5. Study one of these metaphors:
    the highway
    the desert blooming
    healing
    quenching of thirst
    blindness and deafness
    chaff

lofty trees (cedars, oaks)
Jerusalem as a wife/mother/woman
the seed (6:13, 11:1; compare Genesis 3:15, 22:18 and Galatians 3:16)

6. What does Isaiah say about the remnant and survivors of Israel?

7. Find as many places as you can in which New Testament writers quote Isaiah. Study the verses in their original context and in the New Testament passage.

8. How is Isaiah, the man, a model for your life?

9. Delve into any of the review questions or optional questions that you skimmed over during your study.

STUDY AIDS

For further information on the material covered in this study, you might consider the following sources. If your local bookstore does not have them, you can have the bookstore order them from the publisher, or you can find them in most seminary libraries. Many university and public libraries will also carry these books.

Commentaries on Isaiah

Kidner, Derek. "Isaiah," *The New Bible Commentary: Revised*, edited by Guthrie, et al. (Eerdmans, 1970).
    Much briefer than Leupold and Young because it is part of a one-volume commentary. Therefore, an excellent choice if you want to read a commentary on the whole book of Isaiah in less than one day. Kidner's concise, insightful comments will be adequate for many students doing personal study.

Leupold, H. C. *Exposition of Isaiah, Volumes 1 and 2* (Baker, 1968, 1971).
    Sound exposition. Leupold does not deal with application or critical issues. This work is fairly readable, considering its scholarly nature. Most students will prefer to save Leupold for research into a particular passage.

Matthew Henry's Commentary on the Whole Bible: Volume 3: Psalms to Isaiah (Revell, 1979).
    Modern scholars have surpassed Henry in knowledge of Hebrew and the historical background of Isaiah, but none surpasses him in expounding the text for the Christian reader. Henry's eighteenth-century language may be an obstacle for some students, but it is worth getting used to. His applications are as relevant now as they were when the commentary first appeared in 1712.

Young, Edward J. *The Book of Isaiah, Volumes 1, 2, and 3* (Eerdmans, 1965, 1969, 1972).

Staunchly evangelical and focused on the meaning of the text rather than on critical issues. Considered by many scholars to be the finest commentary on Isaiah available, because of both its depth of insight and its clarity. Details of Hebrew grammar and word derivations are left to footnotes, so as not to obscure the main text for the ordinary reader. Young deals with everything from specific words to how passages fit into Isaiah's message as a whole, and he makes a point of refuting common liberal critiques of Isaiah.

Old Testament History and Culture

A *history* or *survey* traces Israel's history from beginning to end, so that you can see where each biblical event fits. *A Survey of Israel's History* by Leon Wood (Zondervan, 1970) is a good basic introduction for laymen from a conservative viewpoint. Not critical or heavily learned, but not simplistic. Many other good histories are available.

A *Bible dictionary* or *Bible encyclopedia* alphabetically lists articles about people, places, doctrines, important words, customs, and geography of the Bible.

The New Bible Dictionary, edited by J.D. Douglas, F.F. Bruce, J.I. Packer, N. Hillyer, D. Gutherie, A.R. Millard, and D.J. Wiseman (Tyndale, 1982) is more comprehensive than most dictionaries. Its 1300 pages include quantities of information along with excellent maps, charts, diagrams, and an index for cross-referencing.

Unger's Bible Dictionary by Merrill F. Unger (Moody, 1979) is equally excellent and is available in an inexpensive paperback edition.

The Zondervan Pictorial Encyclopedia edited by Merrill C. Tenney (Zondervan, 1975, 1976) is excellent and exhaustive. It is being revised and updated in the 1980s. However, its five 1000-page volumes are a financial investment, so all but very serious students may prefer to use it at a library.

A good *Bible atlas* can be a great aid to understanding what is going on in a book of the Bible and how geography affected events. Here are a few good choices:

The MacMillan Atlas by Yohanan Aharoni and Michael Avi-Yonah (MacMillan, 1968, 1977) contains 264 maps, 89 photos, and 12 graphics. The many maps of individual events portray battles, movements of people, and changing boundaries in detail.

The New Bible Atlas by J.J. Bimson and J.P. Kane (Tyndale, 1985) has 73 maps, 34 photos, and 34 graphics. Its evangelical perspective, concise and helpful text, and excellent research make it a good choice, but its greatest strength is its outstanding graphics, such as cross-sections of the Dead Sea.

The Bible Mapbook by Simon Jenkins (Lion, 1984) is much shorter and less expensive than most other atlases, so it offers a good first taste of the usefulness of maps. It contains 91 simple maps, very little text, and 20 graphics. Some of the graphics are computer-generated and intriguing.

The Moody Atlas of Bible Lands by Berry J. Beitzel (Moody, 1984) is scholarly, very evangelical, and full of theological text, indexes, and refrences. This admrible refrence work will be too deep and costly for some, but Beitzel shows vividly how God prepared the land of Israel perfectly for the acts of salvation He was going to acomplish in it.

Yohanan Aharoni has also written *The Land of the Bible: A Historical Geography* (Westminster Press, 1967). After describing the mountains, deserts, winds, rains, and trade routes of ancient Palestine, Aharoni traces the Old Testament history of the promised land with maps and text. For instance, he shows how Abraham lived in Beersheba and how different Judah was from Galilee.

Old Testament Words

A *concordance* list words of the Bible alphabatically along with each verse in which the word appears. It lets you do your own word studies. An *exhaustive* concordance list every instance of every word in a given translation. An *abridged* or *complete* concordance omits either some words, some occurrences of the word, or both.

The two best exhaustive concordances are *Strong's Exhaustive Concordance* and *Young's Analytical Concordance to the Bible.* Both are based on the King James Version of the Bible, but they can be found keyed to New American Standard Bible. *Strong's* has an index by which you can find out which Greek or Hebrew word is used in a given English verse. *Young's* breaks up each English word listing according to the Greek or Hebrew word it translates. Thus, you can cross-refrence the original language's words without knowing that language.

Among other good, less expensive concordances, *Cruden's Complete Concordance* is keyed to the King James and Revised Versions, and *The NIV Complete Concordance* is keyed to the New International Version. These include refrences to every word included, but they omit "minor" words. They also lack indexes to the original languages.

The Expository Dictionary of the Old Testament, edited by Merrill F. Unger and William White (Thomas Nelson, 1980) defines major biblical Hebrew words. It is not exhaustive, but it is adequet for the average Bible student who does not know Hebrew.

For Small Group Leaders

Getting Together: A Guide for Good Groups by Em Griffin (InterVarsity, 1982).
Applies to all kinds of groups, not just Bible studies. From his own experience, Griffin draws deep insights into why people join groups; how people relate to each other; and principles of leadership, decision making, and discussions. It is fun to read, but its 229 pages will take more time than the above book.

You Can Start a Bible Study Group by Gladys Hunt (Harold Shaw, 1984).
Builds on Hunt's thirty years of experience leading groups. This book is wonderfully focused on God's enabling. It is both clear and applicable for Bible study groups of all kinds.

How to Build a Small Groups Ministry by Neal F. McBride (NavPress, 1994).
This hands-on workbook for pastors and lay leaders includes everything you need to know to develop a plan that fits your unique church. Through basic principles, case studies, and worksheets, McBride leads you through twelve logical steps for organizing and administering a small groups ministry.

How to Lead Small Groups by Neal F. McBride (NavPress, 1990).
Covers leadership skills for all kinds of small groups—Bible study, fellowship, task, and support groups. Filled with step-by-step guidance and practical exercises to help you grasp the critical aspects of small group leadership and dynamics.

Bible Study Methods

Braga, James. *How to Study the Bible* (Multnomah, 1982).
Clear chapters on a variety of approaches to Bible study: synthetic, geographical, cultural, historical, doctrinal, practical, and so on. Designed to help the ordinary person without seminary training to use these approaches.

Fee, Gordon, and Douglas Stuart. *How to Read the Bible For All Its Worth* (Zondervan, 1982).
After explaining in general what interpretation (exegesis) and application (hermneneutics) are, Fee and Stuart offer chapters on interpreting and applying the different kinds of writing in the Bible: Epistles, Gospels, Old Testament Law, Old Testament narrative, the Prophets, Psalms, Wisdom, and Revelation. Fee and Stuart also suggest good commentaries on each biblical book. They write as evangelical scholars who personally recognize Scripture as God's Word for their daily lives.

Jensen, Irving L. *Independent Bible Study* (Moody, 1963), and *Enjoy Your Bible* (Moody, 1962).
The former is a comprehensive introduction to the inductive Bible study method, especially the use of synthetic charts. The latter is a simpler introduction to the subject.

Wald, Oletta. *The Joy of Discovery in Bible Study* (Augsburg, 1975).
Wald focuses on issues such as how to observe all that is in a text, how to ask questions of a text, how to use grammar and passage structure to see the writer's point, and so on. Very helpful on these subjects.